Kiss Ma Bell Good-bye

How to Install Your Own Telephones, Extensions & Accessories

Kiss Ma Bell Good-bye

How to Install Your Own Telephones, Extensions & Accessories

Wesley Cox

CROWN PUBLISHERS, INC.
NEW YORK

Published by Crown Publishers, Inc., One Park Avenue, New York, New York 10016 and simultaneously in Canada by General Publishing Company Limited

Printed in the United States of America

LIBRARY OF CONGRESS CATALOGING IN PUBLICATION DATA

Cox, Wesley.
    Kiss Ma Bell good-bye. How to install your own telephones, extensions & accessories

1. Telephone—Amateurs' manuals.   I. Title.
TK9951.C68   1983   621.386   82–18308
ISBN 0–517–54936–0

Author's note: All the suggestions and processes described in this book are designed to be completed legally and pleasurably by any prudent person, young or old.

The Communications Act of 1934 in the United States was amended January 8, 1982, making these activities legal. In Canada, comparable legislation was enacted on the advice of the nation's Supreme Court.

This book is designed to make telephone service a practical and enjoyable activity.

Illustrations by James Barry

Book design by Barbara DuPree Knowles

10 9 8 7

Kiss Ma Bell Good-bye

How to Install Your Own Telephones, Extensions & Accessories

Wesley Cox

CROWN PUBLISHERS, INC.
NEW YORK

Published by Crown Publishers, Inc., One Park Avenue, New York, New York 10016 and simultaneously in Canada by General Publishing Company Limited

Printed in the United States of America

LIBRARY OF CONGRESS CATALOGING IN PUBLICATION DATA

Cox, Wesley.
   Kiss Ma Bell good-bye. How to install your own telephones, extensions & accessories

1. Telephone—Amateurs' manuals.   I. Title.
TK9951.C68   1983   621.386   82–18308
ISBN 0–517–54936–0

Author's note: All the suggestions and processes described in this book are designed to be completed legally and pleasurably by any prudent person, young or old.

   The Communications Act of 1934 in the United States was amended January 8, 1982, making these activities legal. In Canada, comparable legislation was enacted on the advice of the nation's Supreme Court.

   This book is designed to make telephone service a practical and enjoyable activity.

   Illustrations by James Barry

   Book design by Barbara DuPree Knowles

10   9   8   7

Kiss Ma Bell Good-bye

How to Install Your Own Telephones, Extensions & Accessories

Wesley Cox

CROWN PUBLISHERS, INC.
NEW YORK

Published by Crown Publishers, Inc., One Park Avenue, New York, New York 10016 and simultaneously in Canada by General Publishing Company Limited

Printed in the United States of America

LIBRARY OF CONGRESS CATALOGING IN PUBLICATION DATA

Cox, Wesley.
    Kiss Ma Bell good-bye. How to install your own telephones, extensions & accessories

1. Telephone—Amateurs' manuals.   I. Title.
TK9951.C68   1983   621.386   82-18308
ISBN 0-517-54936-0

Author's note: All the suggestions and processes described in this book are designed to be completed legally and pleasurably by any prudent person, young or old.
    The Communications Act of 1934 in the United States was amended January 8, 1982, making these activities legal. In Canada, comparable legislation was enacted on the advice of the nation's Supreme Court.
    This book is designed to make telephone service a practical and enjoyable activity.

    Illustrations by James Barry

    Book design by Barbara DuPree Knowles

10 9 8 7

With appreciation to Bud Ball who provided the technical assurance that everything described in this book will work as promised. Having spent three decades working with Ma, he ought to know

CONTENTS

APPENDICES

LIST OF FIGURES

LIST OF FIGURES

PREFACE

HEADLINE OF THE CENTURY

The story hit the newspapers on January 8 1982.

AT&T MUST BE REORGANIZED. MA BELL GETS A FACE LIFT!

The unthinkable had become reality. The American Telephone and Telegraph Company (AT&T), by some measures the largest corporation in the world, had surrendered in an antitrust suit brought by the United States Justice Department.

The legal actions had dragged on for seven years, enough time for the huge giant to prepare itself for dismemberment. The "lawyers for the Corporation" and the "lawyers for the people" had grown fat and happy tossing pies at each other. The millions of dollars spent in the delaying action was petty cash compared to the $150-billion assets of AT&T and the unlimited capability of the United States Government to print paychecks.

And what did the Big Decision really mean?

AT&T had favored itself by agreeing to unload roughly twenty-two of its biggest subsidiaries, the regional Bell Telephone companies it had created or bought up at bargain basement rates. They'd be peddled off to other owners by 1984. AT&T would hold tight to its long-distance facilities (the Long Lines Department), its research division (Bell Laboratories), and its equipment manufacturing arm (Western Electric). In short, AT&T would dump its losers and concentrate on its money-makers. Justice would thus be served!

The orphaned local companies will have to get new stepparents by January/February 1984 and subsist on revenues from their dial tones, Yellow Pages, and whatever else they can scrounge up in the name of "Parochial Kinship." Guess who will be paying all the bills?

To the average consumer, this is both good news and bad news.

The good news is that, for the first time, anyone may legally go out and buy a broad selection of telephone equipment and install it himself without having to pay Ma Bell a penny.

The bad news is that, unless you do so, you probably will be faced with skyrocketing costs of telephone installation. Service calls, in some systems, have already been upgraded to $50 and will soar to $150 or more if any special problems are encountered at your location. Monthly charges could double or triple during the current reorganization. Items such as "new hook-ups," "add-ons," and "equipment moves" will be billed to the customer at shocking rates.

The only logical and practical way to survive is to *do it yourself.* Fortunately, hooking up telephone equipment in your own home is so simple that anyone with an ounce of common sense can do it. It's money-saving, it's enjoyable. And it's all perfectly legal. So, read on. The best of everything is available to you in this new-age telephone book, *Kiss Ma Bell Good-bye.*

INTRODUCTION

You *can* do it yourself.

You really can.

You can save a good deal of your money and gain immense pleasure by installing and maintaining your own main telephone and any number of extensions in your home and business—and you won't need any special help from Ma Bell. You can accomplish that much just by following the few simple instructions in the first part of this book.

And that's only the beginning. You can move on to the other wondrous gadgets of today's telephone world, plugging them in whenever and wherever you desire without so much as a say-so from dear old Ma Bell.

It's such an easy process you'll hardly believe it. Any reasonably intelligent man, woman, boy, or girl who can twist a screwdriver and tie together a couple of tiny wires can readily install telephones and accessories and thus begin saving large sums of money—and even have some fun in the process.

You can be positively certain there's nothing suggested in this book that's illegal or beyond the comprehension of most telephone subscribers. The new system of phone service set forth after AT&T settled its case with the Justice Department allows you to become your own phone installation whiz. Even the futuristic semi-technical stuff in Part IV should be easy to comprehend.

Part One tells you how to zip through the installation of a main telephone and some extensions. You'll save a pack of money doing this alone because, under the new system, a single telephone installation by your newly organized local phone company can be ex-

3

pected to exceed $100. Depending on where you live it may be that much already; in some parts of the country the price is fast approaching $200.

What you learn in Part One will give you an alternative to paying other price increases expected under the new system as well. For example, soon, if you want extensions added to your existing equipment, the cost for each additional service position will be payable on a time-and-materials basis, portal to portal, as much as the traffic will bear. A routine service call will cost $50 or more. And it'll be charged to you personally unless the fault lies either with equipment you're still renting from the phone company or in the connection between your home terminal and the central office to which you're linked.

But as you'll learn in Part One you can avoid these charges— simply by doing the work yourself.

Part Two will introduce you to the world of exciting new accessories that are only the beginning of a spectacular selection of telephone-type tools and toys. You can get to know them, compare them, and, most important, learn how to install them, by yourself.

In Part Three you will learn the basics of troubleshooting. You'll get enough neat tricks to determine whether any problems that occur are correctable by home remedies (free) or a company professional (very costly).

Part Four is designed for the super-afficionados who might want to consider turning professional. The technical gimmickry is explained here at about the junior high school level.

For most people, it'll probably be enough to catch the basics, do a couple of installations, pocket the money saved, and say, "Thanks, Ma Bell."

SINCERELY, YOURS

And "thanks" is a fact!
No matter what yardstick you use, the "olde phone companye," Ma Bell's, measures up as a phenomenon of this century.

Ma has somehow managed to be all things to all people. A slut and a saint. A hooker and yet, the most gracious little old lady. It all depends on your point of view.

Good quality, heavyweight books by the carload have been written about the old hussy and her shenanigans. She's been a killer in her day. She swallowed up vast numbers of small and thriving little phone companies. She's worked profitably on both sides in all the international conflicts that have beset mankind. She's made fortunes out of war and never failed to profit from peace. During her hundred years she's invented gadgets, gimmicks, and gizmos that have radically changed the lifestyles of millions, mostly for the better.

There's been nothing she wouldn't do for a fast buck but she's never been afraid to work for it.

Until recently she monopolized virtually all person-to-person communication systems. If you wanted to be part of them, you bought the things she made or you rented them from her at outrageous prices (that's usually the case when there's only one store in town). Nevertheless, Ma's untold accomplishments affected almost everyone and everybody's life is a bit better for it. There would have been no phone system without Ma, good or bad!

In less than a hundred years, Ma Bell has built up a clientele of more than five hundred million customers, all of them paying money month after month to communicate with each other. At this moment in the United States and Canada, for example, there's a working telephone available to every man, woman, and child. That's a quarter of a billion phones! And most of those phones have been paid for many times over because for decades Ma has been collecting rental charges, month after month after month.

Let's be fair. The telephone may be the single most personally fulfilling appliance that any of us will ever have. The notion that right now, if we have a phone, we can dial or touch buttons and within seconds make contact with anyone, anywhere who has a phone—well, it's a mind-boggling notion. Regardless of the rotten things that have been done in the development of this global service by Ma Bell, she's always been a class act. Ma Bell's work has not only been good, it's been made simpler to make it more profitable. And that's why we're going to inherit a system that we can manage to work by ourselves up to the point where we hook into the worldwide phone network. So let's begin!

PART ONE

Telephones and Extensions

1 OUT WITH THE OLD SYSTEM, ON WITH THE NEW

The new ways of doing telephone business permit you, in most communities, to wire your home, own your own phones and accessories, as you desire. Just don't do anything that will mess things up at your nearest central office. Then, hooking into Ma Bell's vast network—the product of nearly one hundred years of work involving many thousands of professionals and many millions of dollars—means nothing more or less than learning *how to tie together two wires*. Everything, but *everything*, in this gigantic system of voice communication begins and ends with *two tiny wires*. There's no danger in handling telephone wires unless an individual is very fragile. The voltage involved might sound ominous but the current flow can best be likened to that in a household flashlight.

Let's get used to the notion of two wires and how they work to keep all of us hooked up together. Every phone needs two wires; if there were only two phones in the world they'd look like figure 1. The phone in Jones's house is connected to the phone in Smith's place by the two wires. A total of four connections, right?

Now, let's look at figure 2 to see what happens if there are a total of *five* families who might want to talk back and forth to each other. If everybody in the system is going to be able to call everyone else, it looks as though there'll have to be a couple of wires *from* everyone *to* everyone else. Four pairs of wires going "in" and "out" of each location could do it. That would total forty ($2 \times 4 \times 5$) connections, to say nothing of some kind of signal circuit and switches.

Things are getting a bit messy, aren't they? And still only five telephone subscribers! That's what the telephone pioneers

9

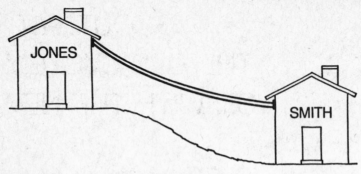

1 / TWO WIRES IT TAKES TWO TO TELEPHONE

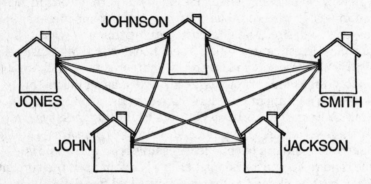

2 / FIVE HOUSES FIRST SIGNS OF A DILEMMA

thought. There had to be a better way of getting things done. Ma Bell figured out a better system, fast. Skip all the wiring between each pair of houses and simply connect each location to a central office, where calls could be cross-connected or "switched" to one another. (See figure 3.) In this way, any two subscribers with wires to the central office could be connected.

Let central do the switching! Even if Jones wants to talk to his nearest neighbor, Smith, it's lots easier to send the call scooting into the central office to be switched on to Smith's line, than to try laying out dozens of pairs of wires as we saw in figure 2.

And hello! What's this?

If the system works between a house and a central office, why not do exactly the same thing between central offices in different parts of the city? (See figure 4.) Nifty? You bet. And exactly the

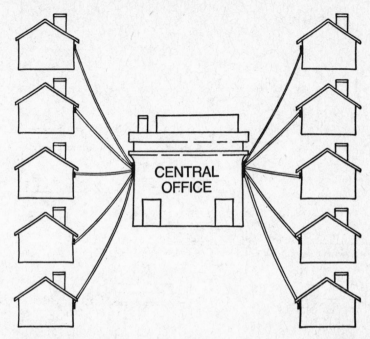

3 / CENTRAL OFFICE MA BELL MAKES HER FIRST MOVE

same technique links cities, small towns, and unincorporated areas—by wires, by microwaves, or by bouncing the signals back and forth to the satellites in outer space. (See figure 5.)

You and I benefit from all these neat inventions and networks. But the simple fact underlying the whole incredible process is that two tiny wires connect your place to your nearest central office. And those wires are yours. They've been given a number. Your telephone number. And that's all that you have to be concerned about in setting yourself up today—right now, as a budding telephone installer.

You can begin earning back the cost of this book this minute by marching your present telephone(s) back to your local telephone store and plugging in one or more of your own. Right now you are probably renting those phones from Ma and she's picking up any amount from $1.50 to $5 or more, per set per month. That's anywhere from $18 to perhaps $100 you're spending on every set each

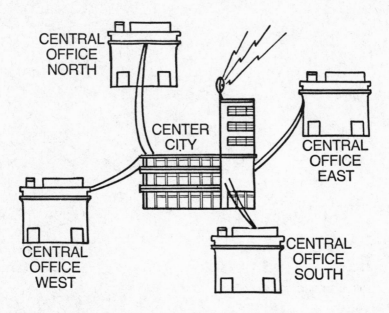

CENTRAL OFFICE NORTH

CENTER CITY

CENTRAL OFFICE EAST

CENTRAL OFFICE WEST

CENTRAL OFFICE SOUTH

4 / CITY SYSTEMS ON TYING CENTRAL OFFICES TOGETHER

year. You can buy plenty of high-quality telephones for that kind of money and get the warm glow of seeing your phone bill reduced every month. You stop paying Ma a monthly phone rental when you take hers back. She'll polish it up a bit and probably rent or sell it to somebody else. Meanwhile, you'll have plugged in your own, bought from Ma or someone else.

But let's keep thinking about those two simple wires that make everything work. Whether you're calling the corner store or calling around the world, everything begins and ends with those two tiny wires. They connect your place with your nearest central office where all the magic switching takes place. The person you're calling has a couple of wires connecting his or her phone to a central office too. Everything else in between is shared by everybody who has telephones, all half billion of us.

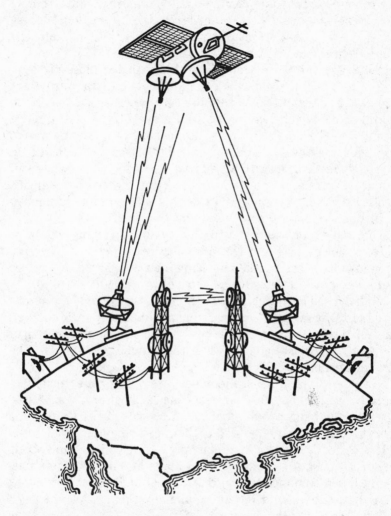

5 / CONTINENTAL SERVICE HOW LONG DISTANCE WORKS

Say your number is 213-555-4699 and you want to dial a friend in Tokyo. His number is 555-2702, area code 3, in Japan, which has country code 81.

So, in most telephone systems, you must first dial 1—that wakes up the computer at your central office—and alerts it that "There's a direct-dial coming." Next you dial 011 (the international access code), followed by 81 (Japan), followed by 3 (Tokyo), and last your pal's number, 555-2702.

Okay. The two wires from your house carried those codes to your central office (where the computer noted it was your circuit at work). Our central office shot the call to, perhaps, a downtown central office, which relayed it to the nearest international office (011), which decided to send your call to Japan (81) by way of land lines, microwaves, and then satellite. Then it was picked up by Japan's receiver station, which switched it to Tokyo (when you dialed 3), and as soon as you started the 555 sequence it dispatched the call to your friend's central office and so to his two wires when you dialed 2702. See how easy it is?

It started out on your two wires and wound up on his two wires. All in forty-five seconds or less from dialing to "hello." The phone company made it all possible by using their equipment to hook up your special pair of wires to the wires of your friend in Tokyo.

Ma Bell used to collect charges from phone to phone. From now on, unless I permit the phone company otherwise, their concern will stop dead at a tiny terminal box on an inside or outside wall of my home. From that point inward, the phone and wiring will be mine to worry about.

Everything that I use in the house, the main phone, the extensions, cables, plugs, bells, chimes, whistles, answering machines, dialers, amplifiers, conference callers, even gadgets to turn my lights on and off by phone—all of them can be mine.

It is perfectly legal for me to buy my own telephones and accessories and hook them into my own home or small business telephone system, as long as they don't do anything nasty when I hook them up to the terminal box and thus make them part of the local, national, and international network.

If I steal equipment and am caught, I can be sent to jail.

If I find it lying around, I should make reasonable efforts to make sure it's in good shape before using it.

If I buy it at a phone store, swap meet, garage sale, or auction, I'm going to be responsible for installing it and keeping it in good working order or have somebody else do the work for me. And I'll be paying my money for it.

The only tools you need to do most jobs are a screwdriver and a pair of scissors. Maybe some electrical tape. That's it. Enthusiasts can add pliers. Super-technicians may want to get into soldering irons, meters, and all kinds of thingamabobs. That's okay. Not long ago, I completely "re-phoned" a relative's house. I replaced the original handset, added three extension telephones, and did the whole job with a screwdriver, pocket knife, hammer, about fifty feet of junk wire, and a fifty-cent box of hardware store staples.

READY, GET SET, GO!

Your telephone is hooked into the worldwide network of a half-billion handsets by two small wires. That's all. And the wires are very low voltage conductors. They can't hurt you.

There's probably a couple of those wires fastened to your home or office right now. If you have a phone in operation, the wires are probably connected to the basic, everyday *rotary dial telephone,* the type that's been kicking around since the early twenties. Those great old dial phones have proven themselves just about the greatest single facility in most homes.

HERE'S HOW IT WORKS

When your phone is on its hook, the weight of the receiver pushes down on a double-function switch in its "innards." When somebody dials your number, the signal shoots into your local central office, locates the two wires that are connected to your home phone, and then sends a pulse of low voltage, alternating current every five seconds to make your phone ring or chime or, in the case of some, light up a bulb. The split second you pick up the receiver, part two of the switch is activated to disconnect the ringing voltage. Your voice connection is then left to carry your message.

Got it? The alternating current is disconnected, the direct current remains.

The two wires that rang your bells, then carry your voice, by direct current. The wires are dedicated to your telephone and nobody else's. They connect your home or business to the central office.

No matter the shape or color of your handset, the inner workings of all phones everywhere are about the same. The plastic cord emerging from your present phone base may contain two, four, six, or even fifty wires. The important thing is that only two of these "conductors" are needed to ring another phone and provide the communications path for your conversation

Although you and I might have no need for more than two conductor wires for all of our residence telephones, it is a good idea to string a phone line with additional pairs of wires when we begin working on our homes. The extra conductors can be used later on for buzzers, lights, bells, even extra phone lines—or "trunks," as they are called—between your home and the central office. A trunk is nothing more than a pair of wires identified by a unique phone number at the central office.

Believe it or not, this one pair of wires can hook up not only our telephones but an assortment of other modern gadgets that connect us to the whole world. In fact, now that many of our long-distance telephone calls are sent by microwaves and bounced off satellites 22,300 miles out in space, it is accurate to say that the two tiny wires into our homes connect us with not only the world, but the entire galaxy!

WIRES AND CABLES AND THE MODULAR JACK

Unlike the stranded, heavy wires used to operate your vacuum cleaner, the phone lines are usually comprised of light, single-strand conductors, each in its own separate color covering and all

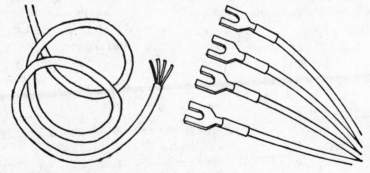

6 / PIGTAILS AND SPADES A PRIMER ON WIRING

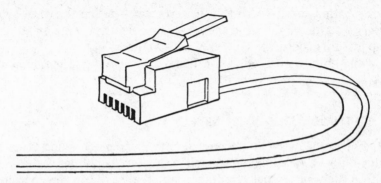

7 / MODULAR JACK A CLOSE-UP OF A GREAT INVENTION

within a colored plastic coating, most often beige. There'll usually be four, six, or eight conductors within each outer covering. Look at the sets in figure 6. Both items in figure 6 are examples of four single conductors within one sheath. At left are plain-ended wires—inside red, green, yellow, and black insulation. They can be twisted clockwise under the screws and held in place. At right are the same type wires, 22-gauge copper, fitted with spade connections that can be fastened under screws or bent over, flattened, to slide into modular connectors.

Sometimes the wires within the sheath at right will all be the same color insulation but the spade connectors at the ends will be color coded. And usually, the important ones will be the red in combination with the green or yellow. Consider the fourth wire as a spare. And usually, the green and yellow will both be retained under the same screw or into the same slot of the all-important *modular jack*. Figure 7 illustrates the single most important device in the system.

There are millions upon millions of these tiny gizmos in use today fastening the base cords of telephones to baseboard sockets. They can be snapped into and out of sockets and moved from place to place. There are several varieties of them in use. Their sole purpose is to connect the two wires (sometimes three) from the phone base, to the two wires in the socket.

In figure 6 we saw raw wire ends—called "pigtails"—which, if you desire, you can simply hook up directly to telephone base cords. Strip back an inch of insulation, twist together the wires you plan to connect, and tape them up with electrical tape or sticky paper. And good luck!

A step-by-step procedure for installing this type of connection system appears as Appendix A, beginning on page 133.

A HARD LOOK AT INDOOR WIRING

Every wiring job is going to be different. Some modern apartments and homes come complete with all wiring for telephones concealed within the walls, usually ending in junction boxes on the opposite sides of the room from where you want them.

Old houses will probably have old wiring tacked around its baseboards. No matter how old it is, it'll probably work well if all wire endings are scraped clean of corrosion. Old terminal sockets are always reusable as junctions as well as clip-on points for modular sockets.

Older apartments are usually interlaced with ancient, old, new, and futuristic wiring trailed in and out by generations of phone company installers. The locations of the original entry terminals are often shrouded in mystery and cobwebs. Don't let such things worry you.

Your telephone instrument must be fastened somehow, to some kind of terminal within your residence. No matter how many coats of paint might be obscuring it, it'll be at the end of your telephone cord. You can open it by undoing a screw or snapping off a cover. You'll see two, three, or four other little screws staring back at you. At least two of them will be holding two incoming phone lines to the wires running into the base of your phone. Loosen those screws and remove the old phone if you plan to replace it. The wires and terminals fastened to the wall will almost certainly be as service-worthy as the day they were installed. Just be sure to sandpaper or scrape them clean of corrosion before putting them back "on line"—that's a technical term. You sound like a professional already, see!

The only wires that can seldom be salvaged are the flexible wires from sockets to phone bases. If the terminals have been ripped loose, or if they've become frayed, bruised, nicked, or just plain scruffy it might be wise to discard them. They're not really wires. They're called "tinsels" in the trade. Essentially, they're little more than a strand of fiber, like string, dusted with metallic material, for electrical conduction. You might repair torn ends by crimping on new space connectors. Sometimes you can use ultrafine, uninsulated wire to bind a tiny hook of heavier wire in place. Try to tin-solder the assembly lifting the iron before the fiber is scorched. Such repairs are typical of frustrations that can be encountered in wiring without approved connectors. (See Appendix A.)

No matter what kind of point-to-point cabling you use, however, strive to make it mechanically strong as well as electrically dependable. If you're using salvaged wire, check it as you go for shorts and opens. Start out with two good rules in mind:

☎ Use the already-installed wiring put in place by professionals as much as you can.

☎ Branch out in all the directions you desire using modern, fresh wiring designed for telephone use, most likely 22- or 24-gauge, preferably with not less than four conductors within the outer sheathing. It can cost as much as a nickel a foot, even a bit more, at your local Radio Shack, Lafayette, Olsen's, or other electronics parts store, but it'll be worth it.

Tack it into place with insulated staples knocked home gently with artistic taps of a hammer. If you want to look truly professional, buy a staple gun, such as the Arrow model T25, with quarter-inch rounded staples, about $17. Conceal the wiring as best you can. If you sneak the cabling under carpeting, okay, but fish it under the padding under the carpet if you can or at least scratch out a little trough for the cabling to lie in peace, preferably off the heavy-traffic lanes in the house.

And again, when you reach the point of termination, think modular, huh? And go for it. A $3 modular socket screwed neatly above a baseboard will not only look better but it'll be handy for connecting and disconnecting phones and other accessories. It'll certainly be more dependable than a clumpy, lumpy black-taped clod of ragged wiring.

BACK TO THE JACK

The modular jack fits into the modular socket which often is incorporated into a fitting called a modular plate.

Figure 8 demonstrates such a terminal. It can be fitted over a standard metal box set into the wall or it can simply be held in place by two screws, the socket dropped back behind the wall surface, fastened to the two phone wires.

Another modular socket style is illustrated in figure 9. This one mounts on the surface of a wall or baseboard, again, held in place by two ordinary screws, the wires fastened behind.

An interesting combination of terminals is pictured in figure 10. It has the standard modular opening on the side, a four-prong connector on the face. You'll encounter plenty of screw-type terminals and four-prong terminals, such as the one shown in figure 11 if

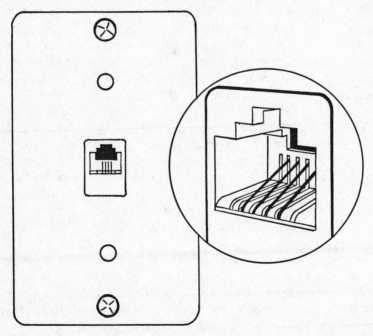

8 / MODULAR SOCKET CLOSE-UP OF THE OTHER HALF

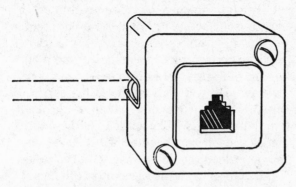

9 / MODULAR SURFACE MOUNT A STAND-OFF TERMINAL

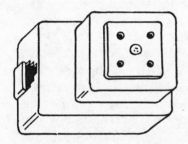

10 / MODULAR WITH ALTERNATIVES FOR DIFFERENT TERMINALS

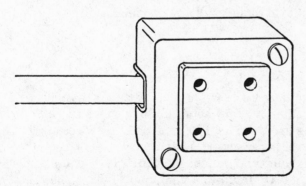

11 / FOUR-PRONG MILLIONS STILL IN USE WORLDWIDE

you're doing a new installation in an older house or apartment, If they are in locations that are satisfactory to you, don't move them. Most department stores and all electronic shops have a variety of adapters that'll enable you to convert older terminals to the modern *modular connector*. They'll range from $1.50 to $5 each. The important thing is they'll provide you decades of quality service.

When you begin thinking about installing a homemade telephone system one of your most productive moves will be a trip through a large electronics shop or retail center like Radio Shack or your Bell Telephone phone shop. You'll be amazed at the number of adapters available (some samples on page 107). You can of course do the job without spending money on adapters, by twisting the wires together and covering the bare connections with almost any kind of sticky tape, but it won't look attractive and it might prove undependable. Loose, fragile connections may cause static, create disconnects, pop out busy signals, and cause other problems for you and your local phone company.

Under the new rules of the game, if the company repairperson has to come out to unscramble your eggs there'll be a dazzling charge for repairs on your next bill. Bear in mind that a few dollars spent now for quality work will be a one-time charge, well worth it in most cases. As you'll read when you discover my pal Charlie, you can save hundreds of dollars using the new modular terminals. Go drape, scrape, and tape if you desire. But the new and nifty little sockets and connectors, with real telephone wires, might be a better way, even if you have to start with only one position in the beginning. Go carefully. Go thoughtfully. Go modular.

TERMINALS

The wiring and terminal devices we've been discussing have been designed in anticipation of a new approach to telephone technology. Ma was looking to reduce her labor and equipment costs. We will get the benefits of her planning. Let's review!

Your local phone company brought the wiring to your present residence in years past. Under the old rules, they then installed all the wiring and the equipment which they had made in their own

12 / TERMINAL UNIT WHERE MA BELL ENDS AND YOU BEGIN

factories and sent you monthly bills for renting the equipment and the access to the vast network of their lines.

Today, things are different.

The local phone company will terminate the wires from their central office in a plastic or metal box like the one pictured in figure 12. The terminal in figure 12 will accommodate one incoming trunk line—one pair of wires. Get the idea?

The phone company will place the terminal as close as practical to the point you request, somewhere on an inside or outer wall of your residence. The central post will be attached by a heavy wire to the nearest secure ground, such as a cold water pipe. The two outer connectors will be your connections to the great big world. And just in passing, these connections are really fuses. In the event the outside lines are struck by lightning or thwacked by a falling high voltage line the fuses will go "pfffsssttt" and any electrical charge will be diverted from your phone system to the ground. The terminal box, no matter what your local phone company might call it, such as SNI (Standard Network Interface) or NI (Network Interface) or DPA (Demarcation Point Arrangement), is essentially the point where the phone company ends its link from the central office and where you can begin your internal home wiring. Ma should pay for it.

A word of warning about Ma Bell. She can be foxy. She can, for example, try to wheedle you out of a few dollars when you carry your rented telephone back to her office and say, "I'm using my own equipment now, thank you. Here's your old phone back. Just stop charging me rental for it, okay?!"

Ma Bell's employee might wheeze a bit and mutter something about a $5 or $10 switch-over charge. Don't let the phone company get away with it. First ask politely and if need be wind up screaming for the manager. All you are obliged to do, in some locations, is provide the FCC registration number of your new telephone.

Similarly, Ma will try to extract one-time or monthly charges for the connection box. Again—fight back. Some phone companies and phone stores will not only give you the box free of charge, they'll hand you a free conversion kit to make sure you get a good socket for your main telephone.

If confronted by a surly employee, grasp your handset firmly in your fist, about chest high. Squint slightly, give a little Humphrey Bogart lip twitch and say, "Listen pal, some phone outfits, including New York, pay customers five bucks for returning their telephones, see?" You thus reach out and touch Ma Bell where she lives, in the pocketbook. After all, the folks in Ma's back room will polish up your relic and sell it all over again at a profit, to somebody, somewhere, sometime. Remember, AT&T's income for twelve months ending August 31, 1982, was $11,859,000,000. That's $68,628 every three minutes 'round the clock. She's not hurting.

If ever in doubt, assume that Ma Bell is still out to beat you for a dime. In the new competitive world she'll have to be watched even closer than usual. For example, if you just accept your telephone bills each month as gospel, without checking for errors, charges for calls not made, you'll have only yourself to blame. Recently, in my own personal bill there were two long-distance calls charged, neither of which had been made from my household. We received credit adjustments simply by asking for them.

BACK TO THE TERMINAL BOX

Pictured in figure 13 is a standard multiconnector box typically seen nationwide. This one would accommodate many incoming trunk lines from the nearby central office. From this point the lines would run to various apartments within the building on which it's mounted.

Large office buildings would be loaded with such panels containing thousands of incoming pairs of wires arriving from a central office by way of underground conduits or high overhead poles. No matter their size, shape, or numbers, these are terminal points. They contain screws or bolts and washers that rigidly tie down a wire end.

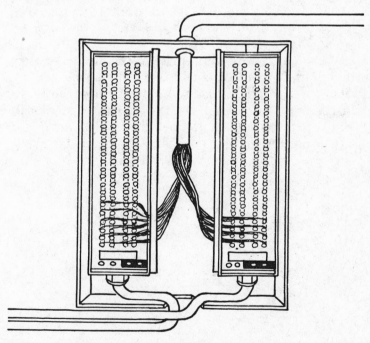

13 / MULTILINE TERMINAL THEY'LL ALWAYS BE WITH US

If the terminal were fitted to accept some kind of snap-in plug we'd refer to it as a socket. The thing that snaps into the socket, in telephone terminology is called a jack or jack plug. Stealing from the electrical trades, the socket is usually referred to as the female and the gadget which snaps into it is the male. Henceforth when we talk about terminals we'll be referring to devices that mark the ending points of wire runs. Sockets will be the devices that jacks and plugs can readily be snapped in and out of.

So, where were we? Let's start at the main terminal, the point where the wires from the phone company's central office arrived at your residence or business. Now you can begin using or restringing the wires already in your location or adding on new cable runs. Maybe the existing wiring in your location will be suitable. It's yours. The phone company has a yearning to get in there and take it back but you know and they know it would not be cost-effective or practical.

☎ SUMMARY

Let's review and double-check our progress. The phone company took our order for a terminal box and assigned a phone number (let's say it is 555-4699 in area code 213). They dropped the line to the terminal and you started running three-pair cable (six wires in one covering) from the terminal through the kitchen, under the cabinets to a modular terminal in the hallway. The important thing to remember about modular connectors is that the wires to or from

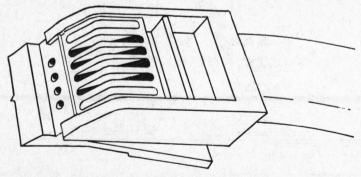

14 / EXTREME CLOSE-UP OF MODULAR GET TO KNOW ONE

the main phone are always fastened to the *two center positions* of any jack or socket. Look at the extreme close-up of this one in figure 14. It's a six-slot connector but only four connectors are installed in it. We'll still use the two center terminals. The same requirement holds true for the socket. Trace the visible connectors and fasten the two wires to the lugs leading to the center pair of connectors. And usually that'll be with wires that are red and green in color, between phone base and terminal socket. If the cable is plastic covered the inner wires may be plastic covered too, usually with blue, orange, green, brown, slate, and white coverings. We're ready to hook up our phones!

The old system is dead. *Long live the new system!*

2 INSTALLING YOUR FIRST MAIN TELEPHONE

There's a dandy little switch inside every standard rotary dial telephone. Between "rest stops" its purpose is to click the circuit open and closed according to the number a person has dialed. The pulses click at a rate of ten switches per second. The rotary dialer eliminated central office operators, who asked, "Number, please?"

The rotary dial telephone was just one of hundreds of astonishing achievements by AT&T's Bell Laboratories, innovative devices that helped create the world's largest communications company. Rotary dialers seemed indestructible. They stood unchallenged for efficiency and durability through a half century. The only things able to stop them appeared to be sledgehammers or explosives.

Nevertheless, high-anxiety people in high-speed circumstances were frustrated by the dreary business of waiting for the dial to return to its rest position before the next digit could be dialed.

In the sixties, again prompted by Bell Labs, the Touch-Tone® system of pushbutton communications was introduced. The modern pushbutton telephone was different from anything ever attempted before. It operated on spectacular new concepts. The differences between rotary and pushbutton might be compared to the differences between mule cart and spaceship. The fastest rotary system can open and close switches mechanically in tenths of seconds. The pushbutton instruments theoretically operate in one-billionth parts of a second, electronically. The rotary is noisy, mechanical. The pushbutton generates tones.

Let's take an example that'll help you understand the pushbutton telephone device and the extraordinary telephone system that we are pledged to protect even while we're playing amateur installers with it in our homes and offices.

Let's say a friend in New York (area code 212) decides to call us at our new number, three thousand miles away.

Using the long-distance system of the AT&T network, he'll need to touch only eleven buttons to reach us out of all quarter of a million other phone subscribers in the United States and Canada.

He'll dial (touch), 1-213-555-4699, our new number.

The number 1 is an alert to the direct-dialing computer. It means, "Wake up, computer, there's some long-distance stuff coming. Keep track of it." And the computer makes note of the caller's phone number as the electrical impulses zip past the recording magnets.

Then comes 213. Ooops! That's our area code on the West Coast, three thousand miles away. But before the caller's finger has lifted off that last digit, the electronic switching computers have decided instantly which circuits should be fastest and most dependable for the best route to our local area, 213.

The caller "dials" our prefix, 555. Our area code computer senses immediately that the 555 numbers are all connected up to the central office over at Main and Brady streets. Zip—contact!

You can see that mathematically there are 9,999 numbers available in the remaining four digits, starting with 0001, 0002, et cetera. By the time our caller has finished dialing the four numbers designating the wires to our house, 4699, it's just a matter of waiting for the next relay cycle to come along and ring the phone in our hallway. That's one second of ringing, four seconds of silence. And repeat until the call is answered.

Well, let's see, it took about forty-five seconds for any good reader to scan that description. On a rotary dialer, the phone could handle the switching in approximately ten to twelve seconds. A speedy pushbutton phone operator could zoom through that series in about two seconds. The equipment would be capable of completing the call in say, a thousandth of a second, if anybody could press buttons that fast!

There's nothing magical about it. It's all just a matter of Mother Nature's speed of electricity and tone signals.

Pushbuttons are here to stay, along with the modular connector, and the new services like Sprint, MCI, and Metrofone, among others, will not be available to you without pushbuttons. Go with them if you can. Rotary dialers and homemade connectors will usually work quite well. But pushbutton phones and modular connectors will not only look better, they'll bring your equipment up to "state of the art." They'll make the extra gadgets, gizmos, and gimmicks described in Part II infinitely easy to add into your circuitry, if and when you decide to leap into the future! The phone company will want an extra dollar or two each month for pushbutton service, if they know you have pushbutton equipment.

NEW TELEPHONES

The economics of Ma Bell's telephones can best be understood by examining the system, until recently the *only* system.

My own rotary dialer came with the service I ordered installed in my residence eight years ago. My monthly subscriber service—that is, the dial tone—was then regulated at $4.75 but I was billed $6.50. Freely translated, that meant I was paying $1.75 a month to rent the instrument from the phone company. Service charges for a color telephone, which doesn't cost the phone company anything extra, are even higher in some areas. During its ninety-six months of service I paid $168 for my instrument, which in fact had cost my regional Bell Telephone company a paper charge of $6.00 to purchase from its manufacturer, another AT&T subsidiary called Western Electric. Not a bad return on capital investment, eh?

Eight years ago there was no way I could have bought that telephone without immense negotiations, paperwork, and legalities.

Locally, today, it'll cost me $2 per month to rent a comparable phone from the phone company, and the monthly charge for the basic service will almost certainly be doubled by the time this book is in print. It will almost certainly *triple* as soon as the company thinks the time is right for such a move.

Let's see what's available on an outright purchase basis. The telephone companies in many areas may now invite you to buy the equipment you are renting that is already installed in your home. Unless it's less than say, ten years old, is sturdy and reliable, it'll often be cheaper to buy new equipment at a phone store. Do comparison shopping, okay?

Our familiar and reliable old friend the rotary dialer, often referred to as the "500 series," comes in all colors, complete with coiled cord, seven-foot cord, and modular plug. Pushbutton phones like the basic model pictured here are replacing the rotary dialers. They're beginning to flood the market, made in Japan, China, and Haiti. Most come with a modular plug. Look for sturdy construction.

15 / BASIC INSTRUMENTS ONE ROTARY, ONE PUSHBUTTON

There are dozens of versions of the style shown in figure 16, often called "French Decorator." Do you want the white with gold trim? Or more filigree? Cheapie?—$50. The "top of the line" in plastic—$100. In real gold trim—$200.

This modernistic look in figure 17 is called "Slim" or "Pulse" depending on the retailer. Several versions of this style feature an automatic redialer, which redials the last number you called at the push of one button. Radio Shack has a reliable $60 model. Beware of cheap construction and thin voice quality.

Does figure 18 look different? It is. No cord between handset and base. You can stroll through the room while using it! The cheaper versions start at $100. The 1,000-foot walkaways start at $200.

16 / INSTRUMENT DECORATOR MODEL

The two-in-one model illustrated in figure 19 works best with cord. It'll automatically dial up to sixteen numbers. The long-cord model starts at $90. The wireless style will cost $250!

Since 1977 it's been legal to own and connect your own telephone, but few people knew it. And AT&T didn't rush to tell you. Regional phone companies at one time insisted on seeing each instrument and certifying it for service even though you'd bought and paid for it. Not anymore.

17 / INSTRUMENT PULSE, TRIMLINE OR SLIM

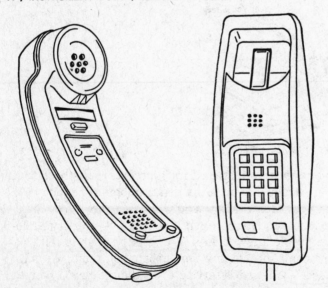

18 / INSTRUMENT CORDLESS, PUSHBUTTON, WIRELESS

19 / INSTRUMENT CORDLESS PUSHBUTTON WITH DIALER

You'll have to check with your local phone company to get some reasonable notion what you are paying to rent their instruments. Some styles, such as the Princess®, add $4 a month to your bills. In some areas, fancy hand sets rent for $10 monthly. That's $48 to $120 per year extra for the style. You can buy comparable units for that amount or less.

Just remember—if you buy your own equipment and it breaks down, it's your problem. You may feel somewhat broken down yourself after paying service charges if you ask the phone company to come out and repair it. In most cases it'll be a lot cheaper to junk the faulty equipment and replace it with alternate instruments. You'll read more about simple trouble shooting in chapter 8.

SECONDHAND MERCHANDISE

Not long ago I bought six bright and shiny telephone sets for $10, total. The modular lines and plugs alone were worth the price. If and when any of my household phones don't function, I'll substitute the mugwump with another one and cannibalize the failed instrument. The good pieces are worth salvaging.

If you haven't got a couple of instruments cluttering up your storage closets already, you won't need to travel far to find some. They're popping up by the millions at swap meets, in garage sales, secondhand stores and thrift shops nationwide.

Will the phone company attempt to scour them out of the market? It's impossible. It is certainly not cost-efficient to chase down one illegal telephone sale. Cost/profit has now become the name of the game, remember? I for one would applaud the efforts of phone companies that diligently go out after telephone thieves who deal in huge numbers of sets.

When I used to go phone shopping, I'd turn the sets over and examine the base plates. First of all, I preferred metal-based telephones. And the physical condition of the rubber feet on phone sets would tell me plenty about how they'd been used or abused. Most often I was looking for a "property of" label or die imprint. I neither needed nor wanted to buy stolen property. And yet I know of no case where any individual has been tracked down and prosecuted for such one-item thievery. That entire question is one you'll have to examine for yourself. Make your own decision.

Another thing. Theoretically, you're required to advise the phone company if and when you are going to install your own equipment. Most store-bought telephones will carry a label on their base noting two numbers, the first an FCC register and the second a ringer equivalency code. Ringer equivalency should be close to 1.0. It's a technical measurement of decibel rating. The phone company may want to know your FCC number and it will expedite your billing changeover if you call them with it. If they insist you bring the instruments in for inspection, you can tell them to forget it.

Now, here's a word-for-word quote from an official publication of the continent's largest independent phone company, General Telephone, based in California, operating as far away as Canada's British Columbia. In their "California News" (Volume 23, No. 1), the question was asked about more militancy to enforce stolen property laws and FCC regulations for the "new" system. Here's the officially approved reply.

YES, WE DO ACCEPT FCC REGISTRATION NUMBERS AND RINGER EQUIVALENCY NUMBERS OVER THE TELEPHONE IN OUR BUSINESS OFFICES. THERE IS NO NEED TO SEE AN INSTRUMENT THAT IS BEING CONNECTED INTO OUR LINES. TAKING THE TIME INVOLVED IN LOOKING AT EACH INSTRUMENT WOULD CAUSE ADMINISTRATIVE PROBLEMS THAT COULD NOT BE COST JUSTIFIED.

IT IS THE CUSTOMER'S RESPONSIBILITY TO PROVIDE CORRECT INFORMATION TO US. INCORRECT RINGER EQUIVALENCY INFORMATION COULD RESULT IN THE EQUIPMENT NOT WORKING PROPERLY WHEN CONNECTED TO GENERAL TELEPHONE SERVICE. WE DO INSTRUCT OUR REPRESENTATIVES TO ADVISE THE CUSTOMER OF THIS POSSIBILITY.

ON OCCASION SECURITY AGENTS DO INSPECT EQUIPMENT BEING MARKETED AT SWAP MEETS. THIS USUALLY OCCURS WHEN THERE IS A PRIOR INDICATION OF ILLEGAL SALES. *GTE (GENERAL TELEPHONE AND ELECTRONICS) IS OFFERING LARGE NUMBERS OF GTE TELEPHONES FOR SALE TO THE PUBLIC THROUGH SOURCES OTHER THAN GTC (GENERAL TELEPHONE COMPANY)*. [Italics mine]

ADDITIONALLY, GTE AND OTHER SYSTEM COMPANIES HAVE SOLD NUMEROUS INSTRUMENTS AND OTHER APPARATUS AS OBSOLETE OR SURPLUS EQUIPMENT TO SECONDARY DEALERS. IT HAS BEEN OUR EXPERIENCE THAT MOST VENDORS AT SWAP MEETS HAVE ACQUIRED THESE UNITS LEGITIMATELY.

There you have it—right from the source.

Unless an individual is caught red-handed swiping a telephone, it's very unlikely any police system or phone company would dare make a fuss about anyone having a telephone set whose base bears the imprint "Property of Such-and-Such Telephone Company."

It won't always be this way. Already, the telephone companies are looking for techniques to "secure" their equipment more satisfactorily. For the foreseeable future, however, it'll be next to impossible to threaten any individual who is simply trying to get good telephone service at the best price.

Don't feel distressed about AT&T, the Bell Telephone system, its management, or its union personnel. They've all had the field totally to themselves, in happy monopoly for decades. Even the official publication of the Communications Workers of America (AFL-CIO) states repeatedly, month after month, that the

breakup of Ma Bell's grip on the communications industry will ulti-
mately end up as a benefit for Big Business, their Big Union, and
even you, the long-neglected consumer!

So there you stand in your old or older or ancient home or apartment. You know you're about to take that big step of getting rid of
that grubby old instrument with the ratty, twisted-up cords. You
trace the wire from the base of the phone down to some kind of terminal, usually seven, twelve, or twenty-five feet away (the normal
lengths of telephone cords). Happy days! You've got a modular
connector. You squeeze the tiny lug on the jack and the terminal
snaps out of its socket.

Ah, no. You find a scrungy, painted-over, ugly little lump of a
box. You mess with it, removing a screw or unsnapping the cover
until you reveal the connecting wires. Go to your phone store and
buy some kind of adapter that'll suit your wishes and, also, match
up snugly with the connector on the new or used phone you've
acquired. You make sure the new unit is working by testing it
in someone else's socket. Or you use the battery test described in
Part Three.

Now what? You start saving money by disconnecting the old,
rented phone. If you just can't wait to unscrew the connections,
snip the cord with scissors and rush the instrument back to Ma
Bell's phone mart. So what if somebody calls you while you're
gone? You're not there to answer it anyway. Now, hook up the two
phone wires or the adapter and phone a friend. Or as Ma Bell
would say, "Reach out and touch someone." She'll already be busy
polishing up your old phone for resale. Now, *that's* reaching out!

MAKING IT WORK

The receiver or handset of the telephone is connected to the base,
most often by a plastic-sheathed cord which returns to its coiled
position when the user hangs up. The truly interesting thing most
people don't realize about their receiver is that an exotic piece of
equipment feeds just the right amount of the user's voice into the
earpiece, no matter how loudly or softly the talker speaks into the
mouthpiece, also called the transmitter.

The wire dangling at the base of the telephone is the important one for the amateur installer. How's it look? Think it's hooked up right? It should rarely be necessary for the amateur to open the base to start looking around. If the phone doesn't operate at once when it's plugged in, you can skim through the troubleshooting section in Part Three. If you don't find an easy answer there, you can be sure it is a tricky problem. You'll want to haul your phone unit to a repair shop for an estimate or toss it away and get another.

The wire connection from phone base to terminal is the key to most phone problems. The plastic-sheathed cable may match the color of the instrument, in which case you can be sure the wires within it will be covered with plastic insulation in assorted colors. If the plastic cable is colored silver, it might contain several wires that are not color-coded—don't let it worry you.

If there is not a modular plug on the end of the cord already, you might want to consider buying a modular-equipped cable before fussing with it anymore.

If the wires aren't color-coded, if the wire ends in the "spade" connectors pictured back in figure 6, you'll see that the connectors are coded by colored paint. Usually, there'll be three wires, sometimes four, occasionally five. The red and green wires should be the important ones. Next in importance is the yellow (which will probably work best if fastened under the green wire terminal). In some hook-ups, the phone won't ring unless the yellow wire is fastened under the same terminal as the green.

Either the black wire or the white wire within the cable (or both of them) will probably be inactive. Unless you decide to use them later for other purposes, you'll be able to ignore them forever. On rare occasion, a red or yellow or green connector will come apart, probably near the connector device or plug. Open the phone base and replace the clunky wire with one of the black or white "spares."

If you're in doubt about the integrity of the wire, if it's bruised-looking, frayed, or patched, do yourself a favor and get rid of it. Replace it. The whole thing!

If you have a Radio Shack, Lafayette, Olsen's, Allied, or phone shop nearby, the salesman there will be pleased to sell you a new and serviceable cord and probably show you how to install it if you take the telephone instrument right into the store with you. Department store personnel may not be so knowledgeable. You won't get answers if you don't ask questions.

Most phone cords are seven-feet long. If you like more movement, try a twelve-footer. It'll cost you approximately $4, complete with modular attachment. Some stores will sell you a twenty-five-foot cord for $5 or $6. Another add-on which you'll find in the upcoming chapter on gadgets and gizmos, is an *extension* for your existing modular phone cord.

THE EXCEPTIONS TO THE RULES

At most, one time in ten, you'll encounter a phone set with more than four or five connectors emerging from the sheath. On rare occasions the red and the green will not produce the desired sound when you touch them across the incoming telephone lines. Just keep switching the combinations until you do get a pair that provides your phone with a dial tone. Then keep probing until you find the wire that makes the thing ring! This process may require the cooperation of a friend who will phone your number until the wires are correctly positioned. Again, remember—usually, the *red* wire will be fastened to one of the incoming wires and the *green* plus the *yellow* will be fastened to the other incoming wire. It'll depend on how the inner parts of the set are wired.

There are, in existence, a few hundred thousand unique, specialized Westinghouse instruments. The pushbutton pads on certain Westinghouse phones were wired in such a way that the phone simply wouldn't function for voice or ring unless wired into the incoming wires with correct "polarity." It's unlikely that you'll stumble across any. Most of them have already been recalled and re-wired for routine connections.

If two or three different telephones all fail to respond to your ministrations and pokings, you can be sure there's a break somewhere between the first terminal box (where the phone company ended its work) and your first telephone terminal block (where you concluded your inside wiring for the main phone).

You can't get hurt by probing around with the ends of the wires, unless you have health frailties wherein the occasional "tingle" might trigger an adverse reaction. If you feel insecure, wear rubber gloves if you don't believe it. Or grasp the ends of the wires in a bundle of potholders held in your hand. The amount of current available even to the ringing circuit is miniscule.

If you'd like to double-check your telephone instrument, glance ahead to the "battery test" in the trouble shooting section (page 106), Part Three. It's the easiest and cheapest way to know positively whether you have a good or faulty instrument.

Again—remember—the modular connectors are almost always set up to function using the two wires in the center of the plug or socket. A second incoming trunk can be fastened to the next outermost connections.

Modular plugs and sockets are set up to accommodate six connectors. Occasionally, the connectors will be left out of the outer slots. There may only be four copper-bright contacts staring back at you when you peer at the connection points. Work with the pair in the center!

☎ SUMMARY

When installing telephone instruments you anticipate dependable service. Frequently, older, long-used handsets will prove to be more rugged than recent models built for a competitive price. A few years ago the accent was on building things to last, not to fail when the warranty expired.

Think over your priorities when setting out to buy new or used telephones.

Price? Obviously, old rotaries are cheapest. Don't be hesitant about unscrewing the earphone cover and mouthpiece. The units inside may drop out in your hand because they were made to "sit" on connector rings while the caps were screwed on. Some are screw-connected.

You can disinfect the outside of most used telephones without fear of hurting them. Use any standard disinfectant with a moist cloth and scrub away at the mouthpiece and earphone. The plastic surfaces will shine well after vigorous application of soap and moist toweling. If you wish to scour out scratches, get a plastic polish from your hardware store.

Color? The colors of telephone sets may be a consideration.

Some people even enjoy painting designs on their own telephones. There are some paints that take well to the high polished plastic. But the parts inside all of them are basically the same, as described in Part Four.

Wiring? It's the important item to remember when you go phone shopping. Keep your eyes open for good instruments, but don't forget the cords. And by all means, keep looking for the units that have modular plugs on the wire end. They're premium: four-prong plugs are easily adaptable (as you'll see when we get to accessories). Through part of 1983, many local companies will convert old connector blocks to modulars without charge.

The items to avoid are those with frayed, ripped-up wires. There's no easy way to install tiny modular jacks on ragged wire ends. Better you skip the whole unit than fool around trying to repair a flawed wire and/or connector.

Again, the reminder! In an initial installation, you can save hundreds of dollars by doing it yourself. If you're moving into a new home or apartment that's been pre-wired for phone service, you can save huge amounts by simply plugging in your own second-hand or new telephones.

The phone company will be delighted to rent you instruments and be responsible for maintaining them. Rule of thumb? If you plan to stay in your location for a year or more, you'll save money by buying your own.

Once your main telephone is in place and working, you'll be hooked. Wait'll you get that first call. A one-second ring followed by a four-second pause. You answer *your* phone, "Hello?" Yikes! You will start searching around for places to hook up more phones. Here's one good example of what can happen to you.

CHARLIE, THE PHONE MAN

My pal, Charlie, is a telephone nut. His home is very conventional, with a kitchen, two bathrooms, two bedrooms, living room, dining area, patio, garage, and a small pool. He has a total of twelve telephones connected. He has two main lines wired to his residence.

One incoming line serves at the main location, the room which ordinarily is used as his "home office."

An extension is beside his bed for business calls after hours. It has assorted silencers and answering gadgets attached.

The other ten telephone sets are of various shapes and sizes, most of them pushbutton, half of them still operational in the chiming and ringing department, all operating on the second trunk line to the phone company.

One of the "main phones" is the base unit for his cordless extension. When Charlie goes walking with his dog, he can take telephone calls from as far away as three long blocks in any direction. There are no steel structures or other interferences in his neighborhood.

By dialing his number from any place in the world, he can get his home-built monitor to check his doors and windows, adjust the temperature, turn on the lawn sprinklers, or tell his television to pre-select a favorite program for taping on his videocassette recorder, certain channel, certain time.

There are a dozen other functions he can control by touching the pre-coded buttons on whatever telephone set he happens to be using. He even carries a gadget in his briefcase that can snap over a rotary dialer if he can't locate a pushbutton telephone. The device enables him to run all his home gadgetry by pushbuttons as soon as he has dialed up his number on any standard, rotary telephone and snapped his tone generator over the mouthpiece. Another snap-on gadget advises him if his line is being bugged. There's no big mystery about any of it. He installed the entire system by himself, mostly from secondhand parts. The basic Bell company charge for his *two* telephone lines totals $14.80 a month. Like the rest of us he pays extra for his long-distance and his toll calls.

"The telephone system has become my hobby," he said one day. "I've got some ideas that'll make this little system look like child's play."

"You already make it look that way," I replied. "I've often wondered what this present system would be costing you if you'd ordered everything from the phone company."

"I can tell you. I figured it out. The telephone things I have working now would have cost more than five thousand dollars to buy and have installed. So far, doing everything by myself, keeping my eyes open for good buys, like the cordless phone and some of the instruments, I've got less than five hundred in the whole she-bang. And it's all mine.

"My monthly phone bill, not counting long-distance, is fifteen dollars, okay? Under the old rules, the rental of extensions, amplifiers, dialers, and other things would be *adding* eighty dollars to my monthly phone bill. That's more than I'm paying now for my TV cable with all the movie channels and special features."

Charlie has an awesome hook-up for TV reception and stereo.

"That's a pretty nifty system, too," I commented.

"Well, don't look for it the next time you come over for a visit. I'm just completing work on my own satellite dish. As soon as I get it finished, the TV cable goes out."

As you can see, Charlie's case of telephonitis is very deep-seated. One of the early symptoms of the disease is an urge to install extra extension telephones in your bathrooms.

Don't say we didn't warn you!

3 ADDING EXTENSION PHONES, NO CHARGE

When your main telephone is in place, you can proceed to branch out in all directions within your home or small business, installing extension phones of all shapes, sizes, and usefulness. If you were to have them installed by the telephone company, you'd pay a charge of approximately $50 to $150 to have a modular outlet at each location. Then, if you continued in the "old style," you'd rent the instrument from the phone company at a rate of $2 to $10 per month, per instrument.

The advantage in having your local telephone company do the work and install all the equipment is that they become responsible for its maintenance. If anything fails during service, call them up and a repairperson hustles over to correct all the problems. If you have a habit of dropping your telephone into boiling water or watching the dog chew it to bits, you might be well advised to have the phone company do the whole thing. But most of the time, for most of the people, telephone service breaks down outside the residence or office. It's a system failure three out of four times. A system failure is always their problem, not yours.

DO-IT-YOURSELF EXTENSIONS

Assuming you've found or bought extra telephones that would attract you to the idea of adding extensions, the question arises, "How many can I tack on to my system?"

The answer must be vague because it'll depend largely on the distance your residence or business is located from the central office, something you're not too likely to know.

The voltage for the equipment is supplied from the central office. It'll always be constant, at the source, 48 volts in the talking battery. The ringing supply runs from 75 volts to 100 volts of alternating current—not enough to hurt a normally healthy person, however.

The greater the distance from that source to your telephone, the longer the wire that connects you. The wire means resistance in the line. The more telephones in that circuitry, and the longer the wire, the more resistance. That'll reduce the level of electricity reaching you. You might be getting as little as 20 or 25 volts if you're the last person on a line, farthest away from your central office.

You'll only find out by trial and error. In most urban locations, up to five or six *modern* telephones will ring joyfully even though they're being fed from a single line.

Another gimmick you can adopt is to open the phone case and disconnect the wires that are connected to the bell-ringing mechanism. (See Part Four for guidance on internal wiring.) Usually it's easier to lift the yellow wire, leaving the green (called tip) and red (called ring) connected. The voice-carrying circuits will remain intact. You might have ten phones hooked up as extensions, but only three will ring. That's okay, if you can hear the ringers from other locations.

STARTING POINT

You may begin running your wires from the main terminal block where the system enters the house or you can pick up connections at the main telephone socket. Take the most convenient route.

Even if you only need two wires now, it is always a good idea to install cable with extra conductors, for other purposes and expansion in future years. It really does pay to start out with real telephone cable, say six wires minimum. Salvaged wires might work but won't be as dependable as you'd achieve with store-bought cable.

The main idea is to make the wiring as obscure as possible. A handyman with lots of drills and experience will probably conceal the wiring within walls, behind mouldings, and in troughs scratched through the padding, under the rug. Most folks settle for something a bit less, such as tacking the wiring as straight and neatly as possible along baseboards, over doorways, behind cabinets and such things.

Don't try to staple the wire to woodwork, using your desk equipment. An ordinary staple just might pierce the insulation and "short" the conductor within the cable.

Figure 20 suggests some techniques for wiring around interior corners, over doorways, and under window ledges.

Although insulated staples are not the most attractive devices, they're available at low cost in every hardware store. They can be tacked into place readily by a few taps of a light hammer. Or, if you feel like a pro, buy a staple gun designed specifically for fastening phone wires into place. Keep the wiring stretched straight and tight as you move forward, using a staple at least every three feet. When you reach your destination, snip the wires with pliers, knife, or kitchen scissors and hook them up as before.

Shown in figure 21 is an interesting and useful modular/four-prong jack plug that can be fastened easily to a wooden baseboard or even a plasterboard wall. Note how it accommodates either a modular plug or four-prong plug—even both! As before, the two principal phone lines will be attached to the center pair of connectors.

It's good practice to hook up the residential system before connecting the lines at the main terminal. Test each "leg" of your wiring as you move along.

Although few people are sensitive enough to feel the tingle that sometimes can be felt through the dial tone conductors, the ringing circuit is something else. Almost everyone can feel the electric vibrations if the phone rings just when the installer is holding a conductor in each hand. To reduce such unlikely possibilities, wire the system before hooking up to the main terminal box, one wire at a time. Or if you have one phone in place, leave it "off hook" to prevent any incoming rings.

At the main terminal block or box, simply loosen the fastener, twist one wire around it as before, clockwise, and screw it down. Then proceed to do the same with the second wire. If you feel the least bit wary, simply stand on a dry rug as you do it.

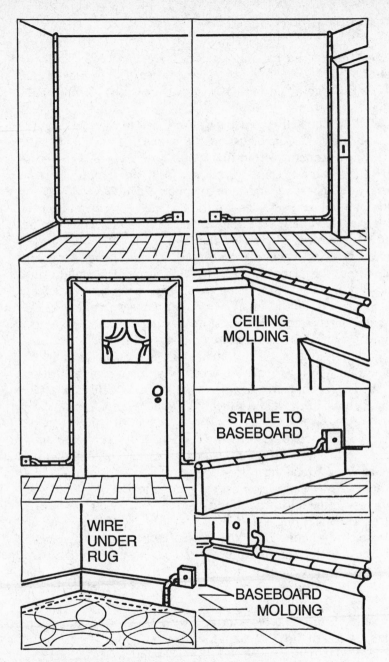

CEILING
MOLDING

STAPLE TO
BASEBOARD

WIRE
UNDER
RUG

BASEBOARD
MOLDING

20 / WIRING DIAGRAM SOME HOW-TO'S ON CABLING

21 / A MODULAR/FOUR-PRONG PLUG DOUBLE DUTY DEVICE

When you plug your extension into the socket, presto—you should hear the dial tone and can make another call to yesterday's friend who soon may be asking you to do the same thing for him or her. You may lose your amateur standing when the word gets around.

That'll be okay, too. It'll be legal. And profitable. And also, ever so much easier the second time around!

DO YOURSELF A FAVOR—PLAN AHEAD!

When you begin planning locations for your main telephone and its extensions, map it out on paper, first. Make a bird's-eye view of your premises, as though somebody lifted the roof off your residence or office.

No matter how primitive your drawings of rooms and walls, you'll learn lots of things that'll save you time and money.

☎ You'll discover how the existing phone wiring might be worked readily into your new scheme of things.

☎ You'll see possibilities of shortcuts from room to room. Even if you have to go out and borrow a neighbor's drill to run a couple of holes through partitions, it might be worth it, rather than tacking wires up and over doorways.

☎ You'll more readily determine whether you should connect your extensions, one after another like a string of Christmas tree lights, or, perhaps, go back to the main terminal to pick up connections for your second, third, and fourth telephones.

There are so many ways to run wires in so many different styles of buildings that you'll be challenged to use your ingenuity.

If there's crawl space under your residence or office, you may wish to run extension lines diagonally under the flooring rather than use extra wires and work hard to make them obscure, going around the perimeter of rooms. If that's a good idea, but you deplore the notion of squirming through such spaces, enlist the help of a friend and his dog or cat, if they're small critters.

Tie a string to the animal's collar, release the little fellow into the crawl space near your terminal box while your neighbor calls his pet from the far side of the building. The animal should make a speedy dash to its owner, trailing the string. Then you can fasten your wire or another heavier cord to the string trailed through by the animal and your connectors will be in place. An extension fishing pole will help thread a wire. Or try tossing a rubber ball with a string on it. Professionals use such devices. Just remember, please don't let your phone wiring lie on damp earth where, later on, moisture may create problems for your system.

Several years ago, stringing a temporary extension phone for one of my own family members, I trailed a length of antenna wire in and around bushes in the garden. I disconnected the add-on phone a few days later, but I didn't detach the circuit in the terminal box. It was months later, after weeks of intermittent phone static, that I traced the line, now half-in and half-out of assorted puddles. And at one point the leg of a child's swing was squatting directly over the half-buried wire. No wonder I'd agonized about the back and forth, off and on nature of the problem. It only occurred when the ground was moist and a child was hauling forward and backward on the metal swing!

I've used a slingshot with a bolt and tie line to launch phone wires through tricky spaces. I've watched a professional use his bow and arrow to sail a wire from point A to point B. I've heard about an installation made by kite flying, dropping the string and kite when it was directly over its destination.

Here's another tip. If I find it helpful to scoot a wire *through* a wall in order to circumvent a long stretch of wire, I rarely go drilling wildly all the way through. As seen in the cross-section view, shown in figure 22, I might do better by boring slowly through the best position on one side of a main wall, then stuffing a few feet of string into the small hole. Next, I'll drill a hole, measured off carefully into the wall of the second room, trying to be as close as possible opposite the hole I drilled in the first room.

Then I can begin fishing into the second hole, using a length of coat hanger wire on which I've bent a tiny hook. I can usually pick up a loop of the string hidden within the walls. I pull it through, tie it to my extension cords, and pull the wires neatly into position.

Using this method, I don't need an expensive, super-long drill.

If I encounter a stud or some other obstruction, I've only made a small hole in one wall and I can readily find another spot nearby. If there's any unusual resistance to drilling, I stop, long before I've

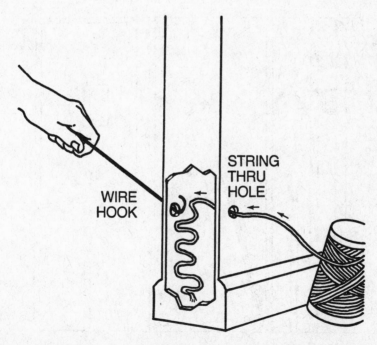

WIRE
HOOK

STRING
THRU
HOLE

22 / INTERIOR WALL, CROSS SECTION A WAY TO WIRE THINGS

pierced a hidden pipe or electrical circuit.

On the general subject of drilling holes in walls, you might remember the following trick for installing modular wall plates. It's not necessary to install a heavy-duty electrical-type box behind the wall in order to add on a modular connector plate. Look at the side view of the connector, as seen in figure 23, part A. The "business" section, as you can see, is just a knobby lump behind the finished plate.

Simply drill a small hole in the wall where you wish to position an extension, then ream it larger with a pocket knife (part B). Most modular plate sockets are less than an inch in diameter. Fasten the two wires to the center pair of connectors, as usual. Shove the wires and plate into position and screw the finished plate to the wall (part C). Plug in your extension and phone your friend!

If you have no space under the floor, you may have some space

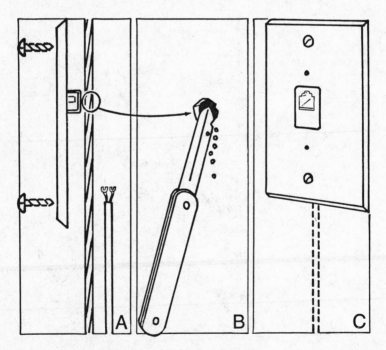

23 / INSTALLING SOCKETS FLUSH AGAINST WALLS

above the ceiling. Look for an entry to it in a closet or end of a hall. It'll provide another easy way to toss extension wires from point to point, if you have such a dandy opportunity for your new activity.

TEMPORARY WIRING

I've phone-wired more tree houses than I'd care to admit. For a small child or even a teen, there's nothing more classy than being allowed to sleep out in the tree house complete with a real, honest-to-gosh telephone.

But I've never, but never, permitted a phone line to be strung from a terminal, through the air into a tree house or across to another building, except on a one-night, temporary basis. If the weather is fair, okay. Hook it up today, remove all of it tomorrow.

Outdoor wiring of that type requires outdoor cabling, with immense amounts of grounding conductors. Trees tend to attract lightning in storms. It simply makes no sense to leave temporary installations in position just because there's an extra phone set lying around.

The same thing goes for garages, barns, cabanas, and patios distant from the main house. Having a party? A business meeting? Got a long job to do in one of the buildings? Okay—string a pair of wires through the air or off the beaten paths and hook up a quickie extension. Just remember to remove the whole system as soon as is practical. Unless it's been installed neatly with the correct indoor/outdoor cabling it can only create problems later on, if not immediately.

☎ SUMMARY

Installing extension telephones here, there, and everywhere through any home or office (assuming the owner doesn't object), is probably easier than installing that all-important, super-neat main telephone.

In fact, some folks who are intent on having lots of extensions but deplore the idea of mind-boggling installation charges will often have the phone company install the main phone, being cer-

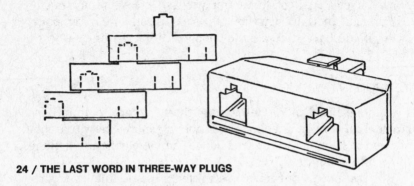

24 / THE LAST WORD IN THREE-WAY PLUGS

tain to get a modular jack installation. Maybe a month or so later they can return the phone company's instrument and simply plug in their own unit. It's costly, but may be a practical starting point for the faint-hearted.

By simply using a double socket or two, they can begin running extensions in all directions from the main phone terminal.

Look at figure 24. It works the same way an everyday three-way plug for electricity functions. It can couple two phones, a phone and amplifier, or phone and answering machine from one outlet. Most stores sell them for approximately $5. Some styles, with wider bars, enable the user to plug one adapter into another, for 3, 4 or more "outlets."

It's a more expensive way of running extensions, but it'll work for you. In a couple of months, the extra connectors and wiring will have paid for themselves when compared to phone company charges which go on, month after month, year after year!

Personally, I don't like "extension cords" that can get tangled underfoot and generally prove to be a clutterly make-do arrangement. But there are, undoubtedly, situations where the duplex jack plug and socket and a long cord on that extra phone will do a serviceable job for a period of time. One thing for sure, if you don't like it after you've installed it, it's a cinch to snap out of its socket and use it elsewhere.

Again, remember—what you do inside your home with your own homegrown phone system is your own business and nobody else's. It'll require only that you're not sending spurious signals, weird voltages, or super-loud noises out on the telephone line between your premises and the central office.

The phone company will do nothing to discourage you if your installations are reasonably satisfactory. The company will make mumbling sounds about utility regulations. But they regularly improvise themselves. You can have twenty extensions in a five-room house if that makes you happy. It's unlikely that any phone company will be sending you enough signal voltage to ring more than five phones under the best of circumstances. You can try, however. And you can dream up your own schemes. Just don't try to outsmart the phone company. They not only know all the tricks, they invented them. Sooner or later they'll catch up to all the crooks who use gimmick boxes and sophisticated gadgets that purport to beat the company on such things as long-distance charges. And that activity is a genuine felony.

If you do anything to upset the phone service to the other 500 million people who use telephones in their homes and offices, the phone company has a perfect right, under law, to ask you to stop being a nuisance. If you persist in devilment, they can yank out your equipment, or at least make it inoperative, by simply snipping your line at the central office, or your main terminal, or any junction in between.

You have the opportunity to install your phones and add on exciting devices at zero cost. Don't abuse the privilege, please.

In today's world, telephone service offers too many accommodating possibilities to let it become jammed, flawed, or second-rate. Telephone accessories can brighten your life, as you already know. If you're not too sure, just wait'll you read the following pages.

PART TWO

Telephone Accessories

4 ANSWERING MACHINES

To get a better view of where we're going, let's take another look at where we are. The phone lines which were brought to your location by the phone company terminated in an official box such as we saw in figures 8 and 9. You ran your indoor wiring to telephone locations and hooked up one or more phones, using the two wires, probably red and green (with most likely the yellow fastened to the green), at the phone connection.

If you simply twisted the wires together and/or soldered them and taped them, you have something resembling a clump of spaghetti. Good luck. It may work well, for years to come.

It's to be hoped that you joined the incoming lines to the telephone instrument through a modular connection. Now you can trundle off in all directions. On page 99 you'll discover a display of adapters which will enable you to hook up vast numbers of gadgets to your phone system. Store-bought, they'll all be connectable with the modular types of equipment. If you use duplex connectors you can simply plug in to the extra connection sockets and you'll be in business.

THE ANSWERING MACHINE

Most common of all the accessories that can be added to residence and small business phones is the automatic answering machine. This is the gadget that everybody complains about but nevertheless usually buys on the first flimsy excuse. The price range on new machines tops out at $300 and bottoms at $80, but the very cheap models tend to create more frustrations than they solve.

HOW THEY OPERATE

If you think of answering machines as basically two tape cassette recorders in one box, you'll appreciate their clever characteristics. When you comprehend the answering gadget you'll gain a quick understanding of most telephone accessories.

So, your answering gadget is plugged in alongside any telephone, by means of a modular jack and socket (or, somehow you've fastened the machine's two wires to the pair that feeds your phone). When the machine feels the tingle of current from an incoming call, it usually waits for a second one, then a third and springs into action. Without lifting the receiver, a switch triggers into action.

First, the ringing relay is told to "shut up, knock it off," leaving the voice circuit clear through your central office, hither, thither, and yon to the caller's telephone.

Second, the switch starts the motor on tape machine number one, which now begins to play your message, recorded earlier for presentation at this time.

"Hello, this is an answering machine belonging to you-know-who. And I'll be away from this telephone briefly. Please leave your name, phone number, and any brief message and I'll call you back as soon as possible. Wait for the beep signal and then please leave your message."

The machine then goes "beep," which causes another relay switch to wake up and do two things. First, it shuts off the motor on machine number one. Second, it starts the motor on machine number two, which is preset to *record* messages, just like any ordinary tape recorder. It records for a predetermined number of seconds or minutes or until the calling party stops talking, a "pause" which causes everything to cycle back to sleep and wait for the next incoming call.

Easy?

As easy as plugging in a modular jack, if you've provided a socket for it.

This guide for free and easy telephone gadgetry has insisted all along that you should make your own decisions. In answering machines, the best we can do for you is to tell you what's available and what you may wish to look for when shopping for equipment.

There is, in this one area of telephone accessories, one style of answering machine you might do well to ignore, even if you are offered one for free. Any device which requires you to cradle your telephone in such a way that the machine will actually lift the receiver before beginning its operations is almost sure to be very old (by communications standards) and a horror to have serviced by professionals.

The more popular brand names are listed below. By no means do they represent all of the best or worst or even more than a small percentage of available trade names. The names listed have at least been in business a few years and have a good record.

DORO	PHONE MATE	TELETENDER
SANYO	MESSAGE MINDER	RECORD-A-CALL
TTSC	PANASONIC	SUPERPHONE
ANS-A-PHONE	DICTAPHONE	EMP
CODE-A-PHONE		

—and dozens of others!

Commercial companies that depend on incoming calls for all their business, accepting calls around-the-clock, will invest thousands of dollars to purchase handmade units. In the residential service however, the $80-to-$300 range provides just about every characteristic most people might require.

There are many reliable brands available, each offering machines at a variety of prices with a range of different features. See the illustration in figure 25. We'll describe machines and their features related to price. The features noted will give you a checklist of desirable or undesirable characteristics for any brand you select.

$80 UNIT

- AVOID ONE-CASSETTE MACHINES.
- ALL OUTGOING MESSAGES MUST LAST 30 SECONDS.
- MACHINE WILL RECEIVE UP TO 40 INCOMING CALLS, $1\frac{1}{2}$ MINUTES EACH.
- IT'LL HAVE NO "COUNTING DEVICE" TO LOCATE STARTS AND STOPS.

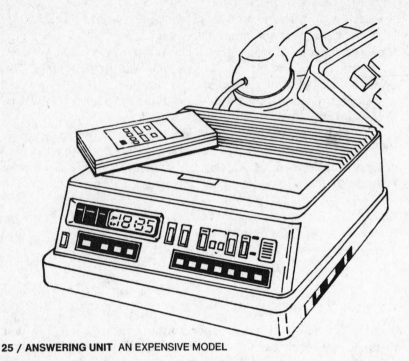

25 / ANSWERING UNIT AN EXPENSIVE MODEL

- MAYBE IT'LL HAVE A FAST-FORWARD TO PASS OVER UNWANTED MESSAGES. MAYBE NOT.
- NO "AUTOMATIC" SHUT-OFF AT TAPE'S END.

$120 UNIT

- BE CERTAIN THE MACHINE DOES NOT HAVE TO BE RETURNED TO DEALER OR FACTORY FOR CASSETTE AND MESSAGE CHANGES.
- CAPACITY UP TO 120 INCOMING CALLS, MINIMUM 1 MINUTE.
- EASILY CHANGEABLE "IN" AND "OUT" MESSAGE TAPES.
- MONITOR LETS YOU SCREEN INCOMING CALLS.
- TINY LIGHTS INDICATE "ON," "OFF," "RECORDING."
- PLAYBACK VOLUME CAN BE CONTROLLED.
- FULL-CAPACITY SHUT-OFF AT END OF INCOMING TAPE.

$160 UNIT

- ALL THE BEST FEATURES OF $120 MACHINE *plus*—

TELEPHONE ACCESSORIES

- HIGHER-QUALITY COMPONENTS THROUGHOUT
- SELECTOR TO ALLOW OUTGOING MESSAGE ONLY.
- BATTERY-POWERED REMOTE PACK ENABLES YOU TO CONTACT THE UNIT FROM ANY PHONE AND GET ITS MESSAGES.

$200 UNIT

- ALL THE BEST FEATURES OF THE $160 MACHINE *plus*—
- DIGITAL COUNTER FOR NUMBER OF CALLS.
- SELECTABLE RING DELAY, 1–6 RINGS.
- CAN RECORD TWO-WAY CONVERSATIONS AS YOU TALK.
- ADAPTABLE AS A ROUTINE RECORDER, DICTATING MACHINE.

$300 UNIT

- ALL FOREGOING FEATURES OF DESIRABLE QUALITY, *plus*—
- COMPUTER-TYPE INDEX TO LOCATE INCOMING CALLS.
- SEVERAL SELECTABLE OUTGOING MESSAGES FOR VARIATIONS.
- VOICE-ACTUATED. SHUTS DOWN WHEN CALLER STOPS TALKING.
- TAKES MESSAGES UP TO FIVE MINUTES IN LENGTH.
- DIGITAL CLOCK RECORDS TIME OF INCOMING CALLS.
- ALL-ELECTRONIC PUSHBUTTON CONTROLS.
- PANEL WILL DISPLAY TIME, DATE, NUMBER OF CALLS, HOW LONG AND OTHER DATA.

You pays your money and you takes your choice.

USED EQUIPMENT

Top-of-the-line answering machines can sometimes be found at swap meets. One of the editors of this book commented that she'd located an almost-new version of the $300 device shown above and the seller made an instant "money-back guarantee" deal for $100.

Was it a stolen machine? Perhaps. But before buying, the purchaser sauntered over to the cashier at the swap meet and ascertained that the merchandiser had been coming back to the location month after month for at least three years. She bought it. It was okay. If you don't know your machine, know something about the salesman.

In this case, there was a safeguard. The seller was not a transient.

Of course, if you can locate what appears to be a recent model machine with a well-known name, chances are, if it's faulty it'll be serviceable. There's not much that amateurs can do when an answering machine goes blooey. They're among the most complicated of all telephone accessories.

Your phone directory will lead you to "Answering Machine" stores that can demonstrate their equipment on the spot, used or new.

My own residential machine functioned well for almost ten years. It began to "wow" recently because the rubber drive belts inside its workings had become hardened. I found replacements for $3. The whole machine cost half its normal retail price when I bought it used. A quick glance into the recording head mechanism at that time indicated no accumulations of dirt, grease or evidence of tapehead wear. Did you know that a metallic tape recording head will generally wear away faster than the tape passing over it?

The company that manufactured mine has been out of business for at least five years. I'd never hope to have it factory repaired. In fact, I once saw a ceiling high pile of the units being sold "bulk" at $5 each. I would have happily bought a couple to cannibalize—except the seller insisted I purchase a minimum of a hundred of them. No sale!

But does the story give you a picture of how that business functions? It's competitive. Only the very substantial "names" survive.

LOCATING YOUR PHONE ANSWERING MACHINE

A new unit almost invariably is given a prominent place in the household. As the novelty of the thing wears off, it is pushed farther into the background, from main hallway to kitchen, to bedroom, to recreation room. Frankly, it's worth running an extra phone socket extension into a closet near the main telephone. The "on-off" indicator light is usually readily removable from the machine and can be extended to the visible area near the main phone. Simply open the unit and wire in an extra-long lead from the pilot light. Use silicone glue to fasten the extended light to the closet door frame.

In such a situation, a quick glance reminds the householder

that the machine is in the "on" position. So you check it to see if the counting device is different from the last time you looked.

A final plea—some people like to load their greeting messages with jokes, toasts, and stories prior to the beep tone. In my opinion, it's one of the unfunny things that have given the machines a bad reputation. Please keep your outgoing messages short and to the point for the sake of the rest of us.

5 AUTOMATIC DIALERS, REDIALERS, AND AMPLIFIERS

There are good reasons and dumb reasons for adding an automatic dialing system to your telephone service. Good ones first.

Persons with vision problems, for example, may be able to operate rotary or pushbutton phones, but it's certainly a greater convenience to locate one button than to dial seven numbers or more.

Individuals with diseases ranging from arthritis to asthma may find it reassuring to know that a doctor or any other helper can be summoned by simply touching one button on the face of the phone set or its attached accessory panel.

There are two basic styles of auto-dialers. The first is an all-in-one telephone, auto-dialer/redialer, and amplifier. In addition, it has a built-in battery device that'll retain the memory system so that the user can readily unplug the telephone and move it to the extension socket in another room without losing the storage of remembered phone numbers. Don't fuss over those technicalities. Your concern should be whether you want to pay for such options, not how they function.

The most basic instrument will store up to sixteen different telephone numbers, making each seven-digit number available simply by lifting the receiver and touching the one button opposite the name of the individual you'd like to telephone.

The storage of sixteen seven-digit numbers sounds like enough capacity until you begin to think about overseas calls or subscribing to the new long-distance systems that have entered the business. Companies like MCI, SBS, Sprint, Longer Distance, and Metrofone are operating their own and/or leased equipment with the promise that if you're consistently spending, say, $25 a month or more on long-distance, their rates will be less than going direct through your local Bell company and her routine interfacings with AT&T.

Another service, called Skyline, is worth mentioning. It's a joint venture of IBM, Aetna Insurance Company, and the Comsat Satellite Corporation, with headquarters in McLean, Virginia. It initiated residential operations in 1983 under the name Satellite Business Systems, SBS "Skyline."

Its SBS functions are already in service for corporations spending more than $7,000 monthly for long-distance. SBS operates totally through satellites. Subscribers call the nearest of twenty operating "earth stations." The calls are lofted to the Comsat satellite 22,300 miles overhead and back down to the earth station nearest the place being called. The call is completed through available land lines.

The new corporation claims its services are more reliable, its quality much better than the microwave group, and with its "Skyline," their system of billing by "neighboring state" versus "all other states" will be interesting to observe. (p. 129).

Fair enough. The same companies, however, don't mention that maybe it'll require an extra dozen numbers to connect into their facilities with each phone call. A thirty-digit number would not be unusual. That's a lot of button pushing! Some systems are getting the long distance suppliers to connect on just one extra access digit.

And there *you* are with an auto-dialer, limited to making seven-digit calls. You might want to drop into your local phone shop or an electronics store before you buy. The least expensive and reasonably dependable machine would cost about $50 and could handle sixteen different numbers up to fifteen digits each. Battery operated. It would simply plug into a modular jack beside your telephone, using the duplex socket, right?

For double the money you will at least double the capacity and the gadget will probably have a built-in digital clock and timer that prudently reminds you of the seconds that are ticking away on your long-distance calls.

They might appear to be intelligent gadgets. Not really. If you have a standard cassette tape recorder and a pushbutton phone, you can demonstrate the whole process for yourself before you buy.

Set the cassette machine running in "record" position, holding the microphone firmly shielded by your fist over the telephone earpiece. And push-button an outside phone number. The tones will be recorded on the tape.

Now, play them back, this time holding the mouthpiece of the telephone receiver close to the speaker on the cassette tape recorder. If your recorder and its microphone have even a middle-of-the-road quality, the sound just recorded will come beeping out of the tape player into the telephone receiver and—presto—your party should be dialed, just as if you'd done it yourself live instead of on tape!

There you have the whole principle of the automatic dialing machine and the redialer. It's a bunch of numbers on a loop of recorded tape. You have to enter the numbers the first time. From that point forward you'll simply depress the button beside the name you've inscribed on the panel opposite each button. One feather-touch will ring through to your objective.

If the line's busy, some auto-dialers will go on to redial without the touch of another button. Every thirty to sixty seconds it'll ring up the same line and then sound a tone to get your attention the first time it can make the connection.

To buy a new auto-dialer, visit any of the major department stores or electronics stores. There are stores in most cities that will have a variety of dialers to examine. Most of the brand names listed on page 61 manufacture auto-dialers.

Because the units are relatively inexpensive to assemble, prices are comparatively low for the plain models. But don't buy one because it's cheap. Ask yourself if you really need one.

Before we examine the span of possibilities, the capacity and amplification features already mentioned should be explained in more detail.

CAPACITY OF AUTO-DIALERS

A cheap auto-dialer will store sixteen numbers, but the capacity may in fact be only seven digits per number. It'll dial out only sixteen immediately local calls of seven digits each! The majority of units handle sixteen numbers with fifteen digits per number. Expensive machines (in the $100-plus bracket) can usually be found with a capacity to store thirty-two numbers with thirty digits each. It sounds like a great many, but let's take another look.

Suppose you wish to store numbers for auto-dialing using any low cost long-distance dialing service, such as Sprint.

	DIGIT COUNT
IT'LL REQUIRE A LOCAL CALL TO THE SERVICE	7
THE SERVICE WILL NEED YOUR ACCOUNT CODE	5
WHEN CONNECTED TO LONG- DISTANCE, YOU NEED	
A SENDER CODE	1
THEN COMES THE AREA CODE	3
AND YOUR FRIEND'S BASIC NUMBER	7
HOW MANY DIGITS DID IT REQUIRE?	23

Overseas calls and institutional systems can add as many as seven more digits to dial!

Limited-capacity auto-dialers usually accommodate longer numbers "per calling point" by simply picking up the extra capacity from other buttons. You can wind up with a so-called sixteen-number machine limited to eight or ten numbers.

You may wish to keep these figures in mind when you go shopping.

AMPLIFIERS

A quality dialer will usually come equipped with a two-way amplifier. Telephone systems carry sufficient power to operate voice circuits for several small earphones and mouthpieces. The tiny voice signal that reaches your instrument can be amplified simply enough by adding on an extra "stage" of power.

Your auto-dialer-with-amplifier will actuate a loud speaker in the unit enabling you to carry on a conversation with your caller even while you wander around the room, going about your routine chores while you talk.

The same amplifier will enable several people in the room to hear your caller and talk back even if they are seated or standing many yards from the handset.

That's all there is to the amplifier situation, except cheap ones give distorted, garbled messages.

26 / AUTOMATIC DIALER/REDIALER TOP OF THE LINE

The descriptions listed below, and the illustration in figure 26, from the accessory auto-dialer to all-in-one units (telephone, auto-dialer/redialer, and amplifier), will give you some basic facts to work from in selecting your system. As usual, each will be delivered with a routine, two-wire, modular jack. Simply plug it in a duplex socket at your telephone (or add it into the lumpy clump you decided on instead) and it'll all start working.

$50 UNIT

- AN ADD-ON, STORES 16 NUMBERS OF 7 TO 15 DIGITS.
- IT ONLY DIALS. YOU MUST HAVE AN ADJOINING TELEPHONE.
- IT MAY NOT HAVE AN INTERNAL BATTERY TO RETAIN YOUR STORED NUMBERS IF YOU DECIDE TO MOVE YOUR PHONE.
- SORRY, NO REDIAL OR AMPLIFIER AT THIS PRICE.

$100 UNIT

- OPTIONAL TO THE FOREGOING.

- WILL STORE 32 NUMBERS, EACH 15 DIGITS OR MORE IF NEEDED.
- PERMITS "ON-HOOK" DIALING OF YOUR PHONE.
- HAS A FACE PLATE THAT WILL INDICATE NUMBERS BEING DIALED.
- HAS A BUILT-IN AMPLIFIER AS MONITOR AND SPEAKER.
- HAS A CLOCK AND CALL TIMER FEATURE.
- REDIALER.
- BATTERY TO RETAIN MEMORY UNITS.

$150 UNIT

- HAS ALL THE FEATURES OF $100 UNIT *plus*—
- IT COMES COMPLETE WITH A BUILT-IN TELEPHONE.
- A "PRIVACY" BUTTON ENABLES YOU TO TURN OFF YOUR TELEPHONE MOUTHPIECE SO OTHER PARTY CAN'T HEAR CONVERSATIONS HAPPENING AT YOUR END OF THE CALL.
- "FEATHER-TOUCH" BUTTONS ENABLE THE MOST CASUAL OF OPERATING CONDITIONS.

Will the unit save you time in home or office? Yes.

Will it prove handy in an emergency? Yes. One button to reach your doctor, hospital or fire department could be handy and the auto-dialer won't dial incorrectly.

Is it worth the money for redial? Perhaps. Remember, however, the continual redialing is tying up your main trunk line.

Some auto-dialer units will work on multiline systems. An extra adapter must be purchased, however.

USED AUTO-DIALERS

As with telephone answering machines, your best bet is to see and hear them in operation before laying out your hard cash for used auto-dialers.

There are contacts and motors within the units. If they've been dropped a few times or operated in high humidity conditions, they might become balky and difficult, even worthless.

There is no easy way to test a used instrument without first plugging or wiring it into a working system. In a store, it's easy. At a garage sale it's more difficult. At a large outdoor swap meet, it's virtually impossible unless you can work out some kind of money-back deal with the seller and get assurance you'll meet again if the equipment proves to be less than advertised.

The other alternative is to order the unit from your local telephone company and pay approximately $15 a month extra for the service and equipment.

You know the retail selling prices of some of the units. You can estimate their manufacturing charges at less than a quarter of retail. Then decide for yourself which way is the best way for you to go. Into the auto-dialer/redialer accessory? Or, a total telephone unit, complete with the "whole works."

And, will you rent it from Ma or buy it from another source?

Decisions, decisions. But aren't they fun?

6 WIRELESS TELEPHONES, AT HOME AND ON WHEELS

The cordless portable pushbutton telephone will allow you to make or take your telephone calls in any room of your home or office, on the patio, or even while walking around the block, depending on pesky little problems that some buildings and other obstructions can cause.

The cordless telephone is a logical next step in telephone technology. The once-fictitious "wrist watch" telephone belonging to fictional Dick Tracy has arrived. The smallest models are still a bit too bulky for everyday wear on the wrist, but shirt-pocket models are already available and hand-held versions are everywhere, as you may have noticed.

THE BASE UNIT

Radio Shack's Duofone® ET-310 is currently one of the most popular and inexpensive of units set to receive incoming calls. The base unit, as in most present-day cordless phones, requires two attachments.

The standard modular connector snaps into the standard modular socket. Now, however, there'll be an additional electrical plug to snap into the standard 120-volt outlet. The purpose of the second connection is to supply some additional voltage for the transmitter in the base unit and also to provide charging current for the cordless extension handset which snaps into charging position on the base when not in use.

This unit allows the user to take calls in any room of the house or nearby garage, even while walking along nearby streets. The range of most units taking incoming calls in this price range of $100 to $125 averages 600 feet depending on how many steel-framed buildings and parked cars are between the base unit and the handset. For an additional $100 the cordless equipment will come equipped with a dial-out feature.

The unit pictured in figure 27 represents the current state of the art in standard-size phone units. The instrument is available in both rotary and pushbutton models. Its connection methods are the same as the "incoming only" receiver. It's a full duplex system, enabling simultaneous conversation capability, no need to "push-to-talk, release-to-hear" as the earliest walkie-talkie systems demanded. The Fanon Courier® claims FM quality, distortion-free, quiet operation. So do most other top quality labels. Maybe so.

Power is supplied in the portable handset by rechargeable nickel-cadmium batteries. Whenever the handset is dropped into the rest position in the base, two connectors interlock automati-

27 / WIRELESS TELEPHONE STATE OF THE ART

cally with base sockets to carry on the charging of the batteries. The handset is equipped with a tiny indicator light (a light-emitting diode), which lets the user know when battery recharging time is approaching.

An additional feature not available in all cordless units is the "hi-lo" volume control which can be handy if Dad is making a phone call while hunched over the roaring engine of a car in the garage.

At time of publication, the unit pictured was retailing for $225 at most electronic distributors.

Most portable no-cord telephones, even the costly models, are still subject to immense problems of interference. Local radio and TV stations can often be heard in the background of conversations. Static, sputtering, and break-up of signals often turn wireless phones into objects of frustrating annoyance. Never, but never, buy a cordless unit without getting a guarantee that you can exchange it for another or get your money returned if your own location proves impractical for good service.

Example? A dear old lady I know resides within a half-mile of a rock music radio station. She is hard of hearing and has a wireless phone with a hefty amplifier in its earpiece. She babbles on with conversations, heedless of the fact that her callers are fighting to hear her words over, through, and between the thump-clang-smash-commercial racket that is always leaking in from the radio station.

I've heard of units that open and close electrical garage doors and others that cause animals to howl wildly when in use. I once listened to a unit that "bugged" all the other conversations going on in adjoining apartments!

There's not much point in discussing used wireless telephone sets because they have not been around long enough to create a surplus market. It's unlikely that a dependable wireless unit could be purchased at a nonspecialized garage sale in any event. Being portable, the receiver/transmitter handpiece gets more knocking around in service. The author is personally acquainted with one wireless telephone buff who thus far has replaced four, count 'em, four handsets.

Number One was lost after he was using it to hold a conversation with *me* while he was working under his automobile. He "hung it up" when we'd concluded our chat and shortly thereafter drove over the poor thing.

Number Two was dropped into the bathtub of water.

Number Three simply "disappeared." We both suspect he "hung it up" in the garbage pail in the kitchen.

Number Four proved to have an internal malfunction. I suspect it was the crystal control that was supposed to hold the handset on its designated frequency. After four recalls to his friendly phone shop, the decision was made to replace it entirely with a new unit.

The wife of a neighbor carries her handset with her whenever she goes out to jog or walk her dog. Her husband, who works in his residence, has a separate "business line" which he switches to hands-off amplifier whenever she goes out for after-dark runs.

She dials their "business number" upon leaving the house and keeps up a running commentary to her husband (pardon the pun) while she's out alone in the dark of night.

"It's a real handy gadget," says my friend. "Not too long ago a cruising car pulled up alongside her. She described the action and I was making a dash for the front door before she told me to keep calm and stay home. Just the appearance of the handset and a message being delivered was enough to send the mobile masher on his way with tires screeching!"

As this book is being readied for press, a local electronics store is offering a brand-new, high quality wireless telephone with push-buttons, on sale, for $59. Brand new? High quality? Pushbuttons? $59? It's an unlikely possibility. This type of ad may trip up the unwary buyer. Maybe it's a bait-and-switch attraction. Personally, I think I'll wait for the $250 unit to go on sale for $199.95. But even then, with wireless equipment, I'll insist on a *money-back guarantee*. No exchanges! Strictly money-back, no questions asked, if the phone doesn't work well in my geographic location.

WIRELESS PHONES ON WHEELS

You may have observed people doing unusual things while driving their cars. Women are seen adjusting their make-up. Men often do their shaving with electric razors plugged into the cigarette lighter

If you're like me, you shake your head and ask, "What's this world coming to?"

Do you feel the same way when you observe drivers ripping along the streets and highways with a telephone pressed against their ears? Less likely. We've gradually become used to the phenomenon. In the United States and Canada today, there are more than 150,000 of the things in operation. There are at least that number of people with names on waiting lists, hoping to get such service. Currently, it's limited.

In Los Angeles there are seven thousand mobile phones in service. In New York there are seven hundred. At any given moment, however, there are only one hundred channels available for mobile calls in Los Angeles and less than twenty-five in New York. Washington, D.C., has a piggy share of channels and facilities.

Even with today's high technology there's been a reluctance to bypass those famous two wires that link telephones to central offices. Now, however, with deregulation, the mobile phone business is jumping off its hook.

You can be sure that within a few years, you will be able to self-install mobile equipment in your car, your golf bag, or boat. Let's examine the present outlook in the early eighties and through the end of this decade.

PRESENT

Today, it'll cost about $2,000-plus to have a mobile phone system installed in your car by Ma Bell's professionals.

Ma Bell will then charge between $100 and $150 a month for "basic service." Next, add fifty cents to a dollar for the first minute of each call. Had enough?

The problem with the basic service has been that the Federal Communications Commission (FCC) has had to restrict the telephone companies to a few dozen voice channels of the radio spectrum, using high powered amplifiers that could reach out forty or fifty miles to find its mobile phone subscribers.

Changes are already upon us. Hundreds of companies are pushing and shoving their way to get licenses to operate in the new technology which has actually been known to the industry since 1946 when Bell Labs came up with it. In major markets, new companies are offering mobile systems unheard of only a year ago.

AND HERE IT COMES

In the new "cellular technology," the current fifty by fifty square mile blocks of coverage will be subdivided into tiny areas or "cells" covered by small amplifiers that might be able to send phone messages for a mile or two.

As cars with mobile phones move from cell to cell the phone calls will be switched automatically, by computer, from one amplifier into the next. The talkers won't even be aware of the switching. And if the demand increases, the cells will simply be redivided into smaller units of coverage.

To give you an idea of how Ma Bell has been operating and why you shouldn't feel sad for her now, let's trace the history on this brief bit of telephone doodling.

The mobile phone had an initial try-out for World War I. The radio whiz kids developed it. Then Ma got into the act. By 1921, her first police car installations were made, in the Detroit area. Mobile telephones soon became another big money-maker for Ma and her worldwide competitor, perhaps soul-mate, IT&T (International Telephone and Telegraph).

Meanwhile, though, Ma's inventions department, Bell Labs, got patents on its cellular system in 1946. After making sure it held the monopoly, AT&T offered it to the FCC in 1971. The government sat on it for seven years, finally opening the door a crack for Illinois Bell Telephone to try it out on two thousand customers. Meanwhile, the antitrust suit against AT&T was getting underway, so everything went on "hold," as it were. Almost concurrent with that settlement in 1982, the FCC said, "Okay. Let's try the cellular system in, say, thirty major market areas."

The Mobile-Moguls-to-Be rushed out to get their names on the line for licenses, deadlined early June 1982. No less than 191 filings were rushed through including one from, you guessed it, AT&T, which wants to have only twenty-nine of the thirty markets. Watch for other names, like Metromedia, General Telephone, Western Union, MCI, Continental, Cellular Mobile, Lin-Cellular, and ARTS Corporation to start punching each other out for area rights to the system. Western Union has applied for franchises in twelve cities. And that's only the beginning! It'll be interesting to see who wins most of these prizes.

There are billions of dollars of capital and operating profits to be made. Small companies are squeezing past traditional barriers.

Lehman Brothers, a Wall Street investment firm, predicted in late 1982 that there'd be close to 278,000 customers waiting in line *in Southern California alone.* A market that size would bring in at least a half-billion dollars in revenues annually.

If the terms of the basic divestiture are applied to the mobile phone system, you should be able to start having tiny wireless phones custom-tailored into your favorite suits and gowns before the decade expires. If Ma Bell doesn't get around to it, Nippon Telephone, an ambitious manufacturer of quality instruments, will.

There's only one "bug" to overcome. The signal waves between mobile units and central offices are subject to drifting, static, and even interference from sun spot activity. They're not yet as reliable as those two little wires that tie your telephone to the nearby central office.

And maybe that's not all bad!

The experts are predicting, however, that by 1990, mobile phones will be about as cheap and reliable as high quality portable stereo players are today. Ladies and gentlemen, place your bets!

7 COMPUTERS, GADGETS, AND— GUESS WHAT

COMPUTERS

Desk-top, typewriter-size computers have become as available as telephones.

It's not easy to list the names of computer manufacturers because their names and models seem to change as fast as their equipment operates. Nevertheless, in case these might spark your interest, here's the beginning of a shopping catalogue you might contemplate.

APPLE	ARCHIVES	BMC CORP.
VECTOR 3	COMMODORE	DATAVIEW
ALTOS	IBM	COMMANDER
TEXAS INSTRUMENTS	SINCLAIR	NORTH STAR
OSBORNE	DATAVIEW	COLONIAL
DYNABYTE	INTERTEC	SHARP
TELEVIDEO	XEROX	TARBELL
ZENITH	NIPPON ELECTRIC	
PERTEC	EAGLE II	—and many more!

Some of these companies manufacture giant computers as well as mini-machines. Others concentrate on the software that makes the machines do the work assigned to them.

GAMES COMPUTERS PLAY

The functions that computers can assist around the home are quite beyond the scope of this book or, indeed, a small set of encyclopedias. There are as many accessories for computers as there are for telephones. The number of programs available to put computers to work is probably infinite.

To list only a few—any computer of merit can readily handle: general ledger accounting, inventory control, accounts payable, mailing lists, time management and control, medical records, household budgeting, and market analysis. If it's an activity of business, the computer can get involved in it.

In games and hobbies, the computer can dish up such things as astrology, quiz games, bio-rhythms, electronic pinball, mystery puzzles—really, an unending supply of diversions.

The computer can draw illustrations, revise plans, suggest modifications, compare apples and oranges, and generally undertake tasks that would have been utterly beyond human comprehension a few decades ago.

Now you may ask what all this has to do with telephones.

Very simply, telephone connectors and telephone lines give the computer access to banks of data worldwide. And because telephone lines work two ways, your home computer can send its own magic calculations to others, humans and machines, at the speed of light.

INTRODUCING THE MODEM

Until now, when we've talked about telephone connectors and telephone service we've been talking about talking—a very intelligent but relatively slow activity.

If you and I are talking on the telephone, the frequencies of our voices might be in the range of 200 to 1000 cycles per second—don't panic, we're not going to get technical. When the computer talks on the telephone it converses in terms of *billions* of cycles. If you don't know what a cycle is, don't let it bother you, you need not know. Besides, this description isn't technically precise. But—just think about the arithmetic involved. Two hundred versus billions!

The computer is millions of times faster at transmitting information than we are but still requires those familiar two wires between your terminal connector and the phone company's central office. And the connecting device will almost certainly be our old friend the modular. Super-computers will require a connector somewhat larger than we've been talking about; it will have eight connectors, perhaps. Sorry, not in this book. We're into home and small business things only.

Between your computer outlet and your telephone socket will sit a gadget called a modem (for modulator, demodulator). It's probably going to look like the gadget in figure 28, a weird little box that sells for $100 to $150 at your friendly computer or electronics store.

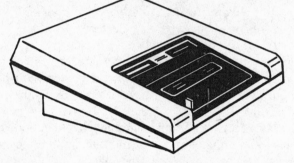

28 / MODEM COUPLER JOINING COMPUTERS TO TELEPHONES

Suppose you've computerized a dandy formula for, say, solving Rubik's Cube®. You want to share it with a friend. But it'll take you at least an hour to read it over the telephone, long-distance, *yikes!*

Follow the action in figure 29.

You pick up your phone and hear the dial tone coming in from your nearby central office, along those two friendly wires. You press digit 1, which originates in your set, races past the modular at your phone, out the terminal box on your outside wall, straight to central office where the direct-dial computer gets the 1 and registers delight that *your* number is about to go into action, making money for Ma and her long-distance network!

You dial your friend's area code, which instantly sets other equipment in motion to enrich AT&T which decides to send your call by way of the satellite, sailing along overhead, 22,300 miles in the stratosphere. The distant city's central office hears its number being called and its circuits are opened, as if by a key.

In the next instant your friend's local phone number goes zipping through to his or her neighborhood office and thence on to ring your friend's telephone. "Hello!"

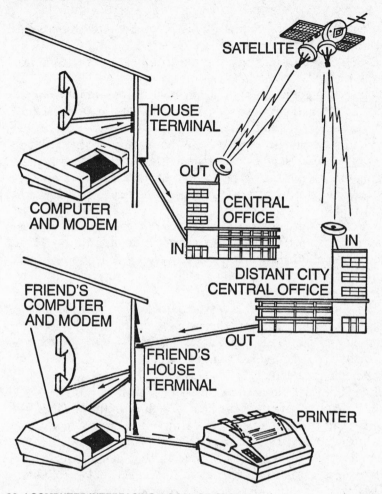

29 / COMPUTER INTERFACING LOCAL OR GLOBAL

And you say, "Hi, this is your pal. Wanna hit your modem for a new Rubik formula?"

Your friend switches his computer to "computer/receive." Or "tape receive." In the next few seconds, the hour-long formula is sent sailing into the computer memory at your friend's house.

You probably have a half minute remaining to talk about family and friends before hanging up. Your call has taken a minute.

If the call has been made at "most favorable rate" times, the minute might have cost you about forty-one cents, though it traveled fifty thousand miles to cross the country, by way of outer space!

If you've never given thought to having a computer in the home, this bit of information may encourage you to take another look at such an accessory for your telephone.

You can subscribe to services available right now that will respond to your requests for ticker-tape displays from the stock market, give you current news reports direct from the news service wires, answer your every request for general or specific data from libraries and information banks.

Major colleges are now collating all the data in all their libraries for data transmission. A major corporation maintains "The Source," probably the world's most awesome collection of raw, random, but retrievable data on virtually everything and everybody with impact on earth. Some computer services will arrange to give you, free of charge, limited access to "The Source" or other information banks, when you buy their computers. Depending on the equipment you purchase, the data can be transferred, stored, revised, reviewed, printed out, drawn upon, enhanced, sketched over, and edited repeatedly.

It'll go both ways along those amazing two wires.

If all of that excitement doesn't stir you, think of the possibilities when, say, all the data at Harvard University are swapped with everything at UCLA, collated and checked against each other, item by item. My technical specialist speculates that all of the major research centers of the world which are now taped could pool *all* of their basic data during the course of five or six working days!

Ultra-high-speed data transmission wouldn't be too dependable sent along a couple of flabby old copper wires. Instead, it will travel by way of optical fiber cabling.

Before we leave the subject of computers and data transmission, let's review the optical fiber situation. The tiny cables are being pulled through conduits beneath our streets and highways as these words are written.

So what?

It means that a glasslike cable about the thickness of a pencil can carry thousands of messages back and forth *at higher speeds* and *with greater precision* than anytime before in the history of the planet. The messages are carried by laser beams.

Instead of costly, hard-to-procure copper, the messages are traveling along glasslike material made of the most common matter on earth, little more than everyday sand such as we'd find on the beach—the same old scratchy stuff out of which we make bottles and window panes. Fibers are more satisfactorily connected at junction points. They do everything better than metal wires.

It'll be well into the twenty-first century before fiber technology will totally replace those two all-important metal wires that connect our common, everyday telephones. Just be sure you know the day is coming—fast! Maybe you'll be the first to be switched over to optical fiber. You'll hear an instant improvement in your system.

And it'll all be fastened together by modular plugs and sockets.

You cannot find a more exciting adventure than a visit to your local computer store. For less than a hundred dollars you can enter the computer age. You've actually already done it for much less by simply realizing that the pushbutton pad in your telephone is really the input of a basic computer. You can move forward from that point in any direction you choose.

GADGETS

Let's cover briefly the multitude of gimmicks and gadgets that you can install to serve you, your family, friends, and business, by way of telephony.

MULTILINE SERVICE

Big businesses will continue to grow bigger and small businesses will continue to proliferate. More people are doing business in their homes. Some companies are having their employees stay at home to do their work on computer terminals.

Inevitably, increasing numbers of one-telephone homes will install second lines as will small businesses that discover they can eliminate the cost of paying store and office rentals. The sociological implications in this telephone "divestiture" are not to be ignored. But that will be the subject of other books.

If you'll recall, when we talked about central office lines earlier, we observed that the "new" Bell company of your town will bring you as many pairs of wires as you qualify to pay for month by month. Each will terminate at a junction or terminal connector. Each line can be handled as a separate system, each with its own main telephone and extensions. One writer among my colleagues has one white phone and one black phone in each of his three main rooms. He keeps the white phone number unlisted, for personal calls only. The black phones are for business calls.

So, here comes another judgment you must make. If you're going to install an extra line, will you advise the phone company it's for business or will you simply have it listed in your own name? Currently, Ma Bell extracts additional charges if the lines are used for business purposes. Obviously, if you advertise the number under business headings you'll have egg on your face if you call the acquisition a "residence" phone.

Business people usually prefer to have their numbers in rotary sequence. If the first telephone number in a sequence is busy, the central office switcher will flip the call over to the next phone number in your series.

And most often, the business person will prefer to have the incoming lines terminate in a single instrument. That means switches and a multiline set, complete with the familiar pushbuttons that say "Hold," "Line 1," "Line 2," "Intercom," "Buzzer" and so forth. They're called keyed sets.

Well, those telephones can usually be found kicking around junk stores, garage sales, and electronics outlets too, as cheaply as $15 used, $150 new if you buy at your phone store. And do you remember when we talked about your cabling? It's usually referred to as I/O cable by the way—guess why? Indoor/Outdoor. Sure, you knew it all along. You're becoming a pro, already!

If you want to move into the key telephone league, you'll be happy if you pre-wired your installation with multipaired cabling. Want to know how many?

Take the simplest installation. Two incoming lines with features for "Hold," "Buzzer," "Intercom" and, say, "Spare."

FOR EACH MAIN NUMBER, YOU'LL NEED 2 WIRES	4
THE BUZZER, INTERCOM, HOLD AND SPARE BUTTONS, 2 EACH	8
IF YOU WANT LIGHTS ON EACH BUTTON, PREFERABLY	
2 SEPARATE WIRES FOR EACH LIGHT	<u>12</u>
	24

Add 'em up, you'll need 24 wires, absolute minimum, not counting connectors to the "Hold" and other accessory units. It can get a mite snarly if you don't plan carefully. Automatically, most phone companies move immediately to cables with fifty conductors.

Your local phone company will install the system for you or estimate the job and sell you everything you need to do it yourself.

To be sure, the good news is that a privately owned internal key telephone system might be a dandy thing to have. Money will be saved. The system can be tailored by any householder or small business owner to suit changing needs, without vast amounts of preparation and cost.

The basic system we're talking about, the Private Automatic Business Exchange (PABX), soon to be replaced by the Electronic Automatic Exchange (EAX) offers all the bell-ringing, intercom-connecting, lights, and routine functions that are so familiar to us today.

If you own the system, you can pack it up and haul it with you when you move your home or business location. You can add on or subtract from it as your needs expand or diminish, without so much as a phone call to Ma Bell. So, how about the bad news?

The task of building the system from scratch is no small undertaking *although it can be done* with only the information in this book plus a little help from, say, your library references or better still, a consultant from any of the hundreds of independent phone companies that are springing up almost everywhere.

Local telephone companies will probably be happy to sell you their used, returned PABX systems. The Government regularly discards them. Some salvage stores will make fantastic deals on whole units lifted out of small gunboats and warplanes. But remember, it'll be a fifty-wire system with spaghetti-like wiring!

Mura Corporation, a manufacturer of FCC approved telephone systems and accessories, revealed recently that in the United

States there were at least *three-and-a-half million* private systems connected into the national AT&T and local Bell networks during 1982. Some of these could be small one-line, two-phone systems. But an entire college in California is also included in that count. And when the Bell's rented gear is replaced by the school's own equipment, it will be capable of handling hundreds of main lines and up to twenty-five thousand individual phones, most of them clipped together with electronic controls, modular connectors, and tiny, six-conductor cables. Let's all heave a sigh for Ma!

For myself, if I were to open a small business tomorrow needing, say, three incoming lines and keyed phones for ten employees, I'd look in the Yellow Pages, pick from among the dozens of companies serving the nation from offices in cities across the continent. I'd get bids. I'd compare each offer with those of my local Bell system's rental or purchase plans.

A small PABX or EAX system for multiline keyed phones comes complete with an instruction book. The main console might require a space about the size of a large portable television set. And wires could be dragged, draped, or stapled readily along walls to various desk locations. If I owned it and were to move, I'd simply pack up the system and take it with me. A Los Angeles supplier, Comprehensive Communications, Inc., recently quoted me a three-line, ten-phone EAX unit complete with every known facility feature, installed, complete, all mine, for $7,000. I'd be able to install it myself at a lesser price, in about four hours. The cabling would be thin, flexible six-wire material, clipped together by simple modular jacks and sockets. Executone™ is the biggest of the private systems, probably the most dependable.

It is impractical here to quote other prices. There are simply too many variations and options to make a reliable analysis. Rates vary from company to company, state to province, even between offices.

Recently I contacted three separate business offices of a private company, the General System in California. Their quotations on a hypothetical purchase were all different except for the monthly charges on basic service and certain standard phone sets. There'll be lots of confusion in the ranks of telephone companies for many months to come. But when their lawyers and engineers get their heads strung together, watch out—you won't have to wonder for whom the bell tolls—Bell will be tolling *you*—slap-happy!

With PABX, EAX, and other multiline service out of the way, let's move to more simple things.

BUZZERS

If, when you did your initial wiring (or used existing lines), you discovered four conductors or more in the cabling, you can readily wire in a pushbutton buzzer at each phone location, as shown in figure 30. Two of the spare conductors can be used to install a simple pushbutton and buzzer on each phone. Each member of the household can be assigned a number of "buzzes" as identification. No matter who answers any phone, a sequence of buzzes will summon the correct individual to pick up on the nearest extension.

THE PHONE BELL

The material in this book has frequently made reference to the phone bell "ringer" or just plain "bell." Clanging bell sounds are

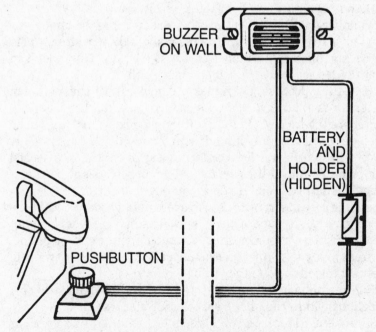

30 / BUZZER CIRCUIT OLD-FASHIONED BUT DEPENDABLE

speedily being replaced by beeps, bloops, ding-dongs, and even one device which plays a different song with each incoming call. An old friend of mine from the Deep South has had me change his telephone bell into a banjo rendition of "Dixie." Regrettably, the first time around I set his machine up to play the first sixteen bars of his song. It became the rough equivalent of waiting for five rings every time I called him because he could never bring himself to lift the receiver before hearing all the music. I cut him back to the first four bars out of self-defense.

And this information may have a bearing on the reasons why many of the cast-adrift Bell Telephone companies are now offering to let their subscribers *buy* the telephones already installed in their homes.

For example, in Los Angeles, Pacific Bell Telephone offered all its subscribers the chance to buy their existing rotaries for $19, Princess models for $27, and Trimlines® for $34. Each of the models in pushbutton style is available for approximately $15 additional. And payments can be made monthly.

Remember, for subscribers who have been using the phones for five to ten years, on lease, the deal means that they've already paid for the instrument any number of times, already. Now they can pay for them once more! One final chance, eh?

At least this advertising gimmick will help cleanse the market of old telephones that have *bells*. As soon as that market has been thoroughly exploited, Ma Bell will offer new models that announce an incoming call with any kind of sound you might ever imagine.

Shown in figure 31, however, is the way of adding in a special chime or other sound if by chance your present telephone can't produce enough "oomph" to do it without assistance.

The same type of circuitry can be used to ring a giant bell on the patio or garage. A "super-gong" is available at most department stores and phone outlets for direct connection into your telephone. It's wired, ready to connect, costs about $20 new. If you want to make your telephone do fancy things, refer to figure 31.

Bring out pigtail leads from the yellow and red (most likely) connections within the phone set or connector terminal.

As the sketch indicates, you'll need to assemble, in order, a circuit with a small blocking condenser, a rectifier bridge, and high

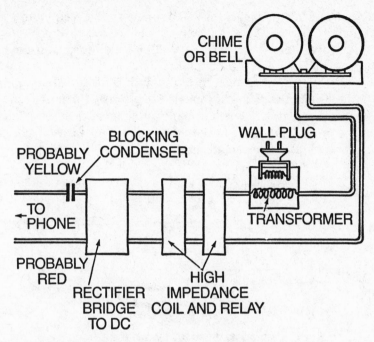

31 / ADD-A-CHIME, ADD ANYTHING A COVER-ALL CIRCUIT

impedance relay working into the secondary windings of a suitable power transformer. This circuit, depending on your wishes, will respond to incoming pulses of the ringer, every fifth second, to beat a drum, blow a whistle, or fire a cannon if the local laws permit. Or it can be triggered for a latching relay to, say, energize a tape loop of sounds of vicious dogs barking. Any imaginative TV repairman can assist you in constructing the circuitry that'll do wondrous things instead of simply making a "r-r-r-riiiinng" when your telephone comes to life.

CONFERENCE CALLS AND FORWARDING

Multiline phone users, even single-line householders, can install gadgets costing about $50 new which can enable the owner to connect with two or three other phones at the same time.

Once in position, using modular connectors, the dialer simply calls on the device to dial the selected numbers and feed them all into one line.

Thus, Aunt Jane can talk to Uncle Bill, little Mary, and their friendly astrologer all at the same time.

The conference caller seen in figure 32 has an added feature. It'll cost extra money. If Aunt Jane decides to visit Uncle Bill, she can simply punch in Uncle Bill's phone number before leaving her home and any calls made to her number will be "forwarded" along to her at Uncle Bill's, automatically.

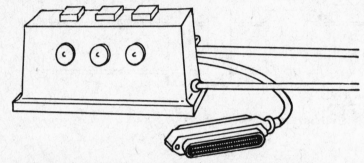

32 / CONFERENCE CALLER/FORWARDER YOU MIGHT PREFER MA'S

Don't buy this equipment however, before checking with your local telephone company. Progressive local companies can add this facility to your present phone line on a monthly rental basis. Early indications are that the cost will be modest, particularly if the add-on can be done by a technician within the central office, without having to visit your home.

AMPLIFIERS

Consider buying an amplifier if there are hearing-impaired persons involved in your life. A simple amplifier such as shown in figure 33 will plug in, form a parallel circuit with the phone, and will have a switch which enables the whole room to be filled with the sound of the incoming caller's voice. Any number of people can talk back and forth in a hands-off conference-style call although no telephones will be in use, assuming the incoming caller is similarly equipped.

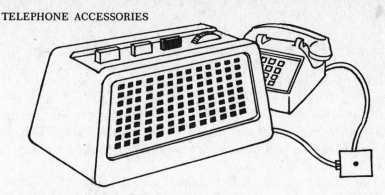

33 / ROOM-TYPE PHONE AMPLIFIER "SQUAWK BOX"

For the hearing-impaired, you can install an amplifier-receiver without a "squawk box," as the loud speakers are known. A small button on top of the handset enables the listener to turn the volume up or down on the receiver of the telephone.

When you talk through any ordinary telephone, a certain balanced amount of your call is simultaneously being heard through your earpiece. It's a "side-tone" in technical jargon.

But you may not appreciate it until you stifle the sound in your own earphone. You'll be surprised how eerie it sounds when you can't hear the sound of your own voice coming back through your earpiece as you speak. It'll give you an incentive to provide an amplifying handpiece for anyone you know who is hard of hearing.

POTPOURRI OF TELEPHONE ACCESSORIES

Telephone stores and phone shops run by Ma will offer you a bewildering assortment of interesting, if rather unnecessary gadgetry for your telephone usage.

Switches are available to shut off the ringing sound altogether. Others are available that snap in place and make it easy to adjust the level without having to turn the set upside down and fumble for the bell control.

There are battery-driven indexes to list numbers and names and addresses. And you might enjoy having one of the many styles of clip-on things that enable you to rest the receiver against your shoulder while you use your hands for other work or play. And there are even solid-gold caps that clip over your handset to give a monogram ornamentation. Another gizmo that can be plugged in or simply stuck on to a handset will enable you to tape record conversations if you have a cassette recorder. A snap-on amplifier boosts the speaker's voice as much as five times normal. Another plastic attachment can be carried in your pocket but when clipped over a mouthpiece will tell you by visual signal if there is any "bug" on the line or if anyone else is eavesdropping your conversation on an extension.

All of these are available right now at your friendly phone store.

There's a device which is just reaching the market, barely out of test stage, which will automatically dial your local police and announce that a burglary is in process. It can be fastened into a professional security system. Not too many police departments are yet willing to go for the tape loop alarm, however. The frequency of false alarms is still proving too high for most of them.

THE CURRENT ULTIMATE ACCESSORY

The BSR X-10 system is the first mass-produced version of an accessory that has been operating on a homemade basis in the homes of telephone buffs for many years. Now, at last it's been refined to the point where anybody can own one and attach it in seconds to their residential phone system. The BSR system enables you to protect and control your home and all electro-mechanical devices within it from any telephone, anywhere in the world.

The X-10 unit seen in figure 34 is limited to eight basic control functions, but can readily be advanced to perform ninety-nine functions with a simple bit of reworking by any alert electronics technician.

In the terms of this free and easy phone book, it's rather expensive. In terms of your needs and wants, it may be the most exciting add-on that's entered the telephone field for many years.

The large unit is the base station that plugs into two sockets in your home. One plug is inserted in an electrical outlet, the other, in our ever-popular telephone duplex jack. You decide which functions you'd like to control by telephone calls.

If you decide on telephoning the living room lamp, the radio, the TV/videocassette recorder, microwave oven, you simply insert

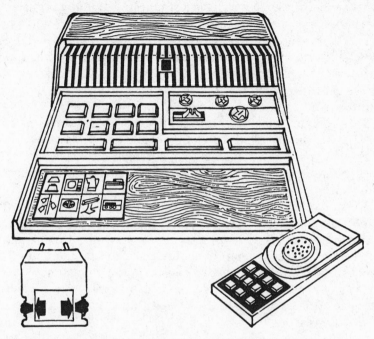

34 / BSR X-10 AT PRESENT, AN ULTIMATE ACCESSORY

modules (supplied with the system) in the sockets where those items are now plugged, making note of which module is in which socket, controlling which appliance.

That's it! You're ready. You toss the tiny remote transmitter into your pocket and off you go to work or a trip around the world.

Let's suppose you have placed a module into your BSR X-10 that will enable you to reach your answering machine monitor. You've placed that module in position 4, let us say.

Later in the day, you dial your home. The answering machine responds and you hold your remote unit up to the telephone at your calling position and depress button 4.

For the next period of preset time, the answering machine monitor will deliver to you all the calls that reached your home during your absence. Dial position 5 and it'll cut in a microphone to relay anything happening *right now* in your house.

You can also arrange to have it report to you if any of the windows or doors have opened while you were away, because it's tied in to your home security system!

Before hanging up, you may decide to turn on the oven, (push button 6) turn on the outdoor lights (button 8) and instruct the TV/videocassette recorder to tape the channel 3 show at 6:00 P.M. (button 9).

The machine will signal you a positive note when these instructions have been received. You hang up and go on your way.

By now you know that if you can accomplish this piece of business from your office, you can do exactly the same things by dialing into your home from the opposite side of the world.

Expensive? As already noted, it's not free. The basic unit with remote transmitter sells for $125. Each operations module will cost between $15 and $25, depending on the amount of amperage it must control in your home. The cheap unit can control a lamp. The expensive one might be needed to, say, start a big motor.

Let's get back to your basic telephone system!

THE GADGETRY SHOP

All the good things seen in figure 35 are available now at local department stores, radio/telephone stores, and electronics supply houses in most communities. The prices shown are for the most part "top-of-the-line" high retail. If you haven't got a "connection" for wholesale prices, shop around local electronics stores and be flat-out honest saying you hope to get "net" prices allowed to most technicians. Obviously if you're only going to buy one or two items, it won't be worth the effort. Let's see some of the components you might desire.

A. QUICK PLUG
CONVERTS OLD PHONES FOR MODULAR JACKS $2.50
B. DUPLEX JACK
ENABLES TWO JACKS TO ENTER ONE OUTLET 5.00
C. MODULAR SOCKET
A "TERMINAL SOCKET" FOR THE WALL 5.00
D. MOD-MOD CORDS
REPLACEMENT CORDS FOR YOUR PHONE: 7 FEET 3.00
12 FEET 4.00
25 FEET 6.00

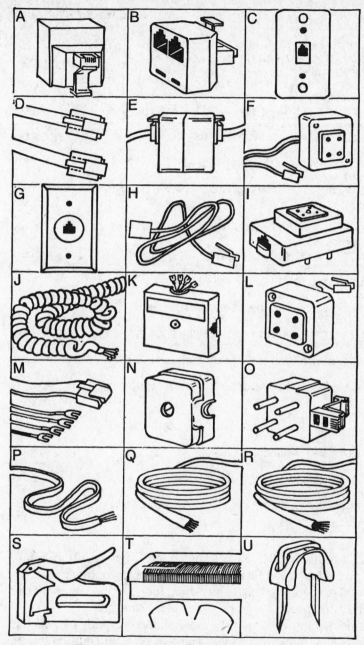

E. IN-LINE COUPLERS
INTERCONNECTS 2 JACK PLUGS   2.50
F. PLUG ADAPTER
CONVERTS 4-PRONG TO MODULAR SOCKET   4.00
G. WALL PLATE
TO MAKE THE TERMINAL FLUSH TO WALL   5.00
H. EXTENSION CORDS
TO ADD LENGTH TO EXISTING CORDS   25 FEET 4.00
I. INSTANT JACK
CONVERTS 4-PRONG TO MODULAR JACK   5.00
J. HANDSET CORD
COILED WIRE REPLACEMENT FROM BASE INTO HAND-
PIECE   4.00
K. QUICK CONNECT
SURFACE MOUNTED, SCREW FASTENERS   5.00
L. JACK AND PLUG
CONNECTS TWO PHONES TO ONE JACK   6.00
M. CONVERTER CORD
MODULAR ONE END, TERMINALS OTHER   4.00
N. TERMINAL
OLD-TYPE SCREW BOX. JUNCTION FOR CORDS   2.00
O. PLUG
TO MATE WITH 4-PRONG *AND* MODULAR SOCKETS   4.00
P. FLEX
50 FEET, SATIN FINISH, 4 CONDUCTOR CABLING   2.50
Q. SOLID
100 FEET, SOLID CONDUCTORS. 6 IN SHEATH, COL-
ORED   5.00
R. SOLID
100 FEET, ROUND PHONE CABLE, 6 CONDUCTOR,
BEIGE   7.00
S. INSTALLATION STAPLE GUN   17.00
T. STAPLES
PACKAGES OF 1,000   2.50
U. INSULATED STAPLES
FOR HAMMERING, FASTENING CABLE TO WALLS, ETC.
50 FOR   1.00

Again, a reminder. The prices shown are single-unit high retail. Almost any telephone installer, TV technician, or student trades-man would probably be able to buy them for 50 or 75 percent of the prices indicated, with further discounts for quantity.

Have no hesitation to visit the local phone company installation office. They have all kinds of tools, gadgets, odds and ends of things that they'll sell to you (in most locations) just as readily as they'll assign them to the employees who load up their installation trucks for each day's work.

And if there's something puzzling you about an instrument, device or installation, for heaven's sake, *ask* a nearby technician. There will always be the gruff employee who won't want to be helpful. In most cases, however, if you ask politely, any of Ma's employees will answer you thoughtfully and cordially.

You may feel confused by all this gobbleydegook!

Can you do it? Of course you can.

All you need is a determination to have some fun!

If you can snap a modular telephone jack into its socket, you can certainly do the same with a modular device to control appliances. And you can install the wires and sockets, too! Your telephone provides security, convenience, and pleasure. And best of all, if you decide to have equipment even as fancy as the X-10, it'll be yours, all yours. You will not be paying substantial charges to rent the thing from month to month. Shop for other brands and prices before buying almost everything in telephones.

GUESS WHAT

You've become an expert in the telephone installation game.

More than likely, for openers you've decided to stop paying monthly rentals for your telephone handsets and have either located some better or cheaper models at department stores, swap meets, and/or your local telephone mart. Or you've made a deal with Ma for the stuff you have now.

From the beginning we said we would tell you all you needed to know about hooking up the two wires that connect your home or business with all of the great big outside world.

That much has been done. There's really nothing more to know.

There are two wires connecting your main phone via a terminal box to your central office. You've run extensions to the locations where you wanted them, testing each of them as you went along. You've added the gadgets that sounded appealing to you. In the process, you've probably made a substantial reduction in your monthly phone bill. If the full benefit of the saving isn't felt immediately, at least you have the satisfaction of knowing the equipment is yours. You'll not be paying, paying, paying, forever, the monthly rental charge that would have been required of you under the old system.

If you bought a $5 swap meet telephone, its cost will be offset in two or three months. If you went the distance and bought a "decorator fancy," the advantages may not be felt for a bit longer.

With everyday routine care and concern, your telephone equipment should function flawlessly year after year.

The minimum life of the average table-top phone is accepted as roughly twenty years. Our own technical expert, Bud Ball, phoned a half dozen of his acquaintances in Ma Bell companies coast to coast and reported back that in their opinion, residential service calls occur for most householders probably once each decade. And then, the trouble is usually caused by accident rather than casual use.

If something goes wrong, you'll soon figure out whether the fault lies in your wiring, your equipment, or with the phone company. The trouble shooting section of this book begins on the next page.

And if Part Four doesn't exactly make you the world's foremost expert, if you learn to use some of the words correctly, at least you'll sound like you're a pro. I hope you've had fun this far. See you on the next page. . . .

PART THREE

Trouble Shooting

8 IN CASE YOU EVER HAVE TROUBLE

There are many activities in which the amateur does better work than the professional. Most dedicated amateur car mechanics drive cars that function better than the comparable models that are hustled in and out of dealer repair shops. Furniture refinishings, dressmaking and house painting are other routine examples in which keenly motivated amateurs get better results than their production-line counterparts.

If things don't go perfectly the first time, any good amateur will keep at the problem until he gets it right. The professional is often required to press ahead to the next job on a tight schedule. Amateurs usually take an extra pride in their efforts and results. Professionals will all too often be satisfied if they're not called back by disappointed customers or irate bosses.

So that's why homemade telephone installations are routinely done better than comparable work performed by professionals. We're talking of course about the "entry-level" type of phone installations. Despite care and thoughtfulness, however, glitches can pop up in our routine telephone service.

WE WANT TO AVOID TROUBLES

Whenever you or I decide to install our own phone systems and gadgetry, we do so with the idea of saving money, adding to our pleasure by adding to our facilities, or both.

We start out with the notion that we'll do things right.

First, we want to hook up dependable, fault-free equipment. Second, we want to avoid the annoyance and time-consuming frustrations of trouble shooting. If we install faulty equipment or sloppy wiring or use it all in a haphazard way, chances are we'll be busy correcting our oversights, sooner or later.

There's a third and very important reason to do it carefully. We just happen to have inherited a remarkably good nationwide communications system. The minute we fasten our two wires from residence or office to the terminal or entry box brought to our premises by the phone company, we become part of a global network of elegant facilities which we should respect and maintain.

If we do sloppy work we can expect sloppy service. If that poor work interferes with the system, the phone company will simply disconnect us as their central office if we don't correct our problems. Snip!

Our basic concern of course is always going to be—is the problem on my side of that terminal box or their side?

BEGIN AT THE BEGINNING

There's no scientific basis for the statement but most professionals will agree that most telephone troubles are located *outside* the residential user's location.

Forget for a minute the nerd who regularly leaves his or her telephone off its hook. Skip the sloppy homeowner who can destroy cords as fast as an installer can replace them. In the well-tempered household, telephone service rarely fails. In your own homemade installation there'll be virtually no problems if there's been some tender, loving attention to details as each step is taken.

If you're going to get into the action, start confidently.

The Tools. You'll need a decent screwdriver or two, a pair of pliers, some tape, a pocket knife, hammer and staples or staple gun for cabling.

The Planning. Scratch out a diagram on a pad of paper. No matter how old, your existing house wiring will be useable. You'll be adding to it. Think ahead about equipment you may buy later and plan now how you'll run cabling to plug it in.

The Equipment. During the first few years of divestiture, new and used equipment will be flooding the market. Make contact with several suppliers and buy from those who are able to give you top quality at the most favorable prices. Look for quality brand names that you can rely on. It won't take you long to discover the good ones.

Test Equipment. With the few gadgets shown in figures 36, 37, and 38, you should be able to work in and out of all known prob-

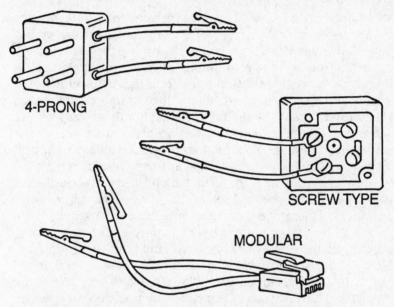

4-PRONG

SCREW TYPE

MODULAR

36 / TEST EQUIPMENT PRONG, MODULAR, FOUR-SCREW ADAPTERS

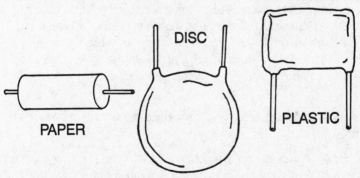

DISC

PLASTIC

PAPER

37 / TEST AND SET EQUIPMENT TYPES OF CONDENSERS

lems. Each of the pieces in figure 36 has a few "alligator clips" that enable you to fasten readily onto operating circuits or assorted plugs. I asked a TV technician to make up a set such as shown in figure 36 for me to pass along to a relative who expects to go into the telephone installation business when he retires next year. The TV man made up these units from his "junk box" and charged me $6 for all of it.

You'll encounter the word *condensers* frequently in telephony. Here are three typical "caps," as they're called by the professionals. Condensers have a capability of stopping the passage of direct current from point to point. But they permit the "pressure" of that voltage to be felt, electronically, from one connector to the other. Sometimes they'll "short" or go "open," almost half the time the reason for failures in ringing systems. Routinely they sell for about twenty-five cents each. If ever in doubt about electricity when testing a circuit, slip a condenser into the alligator clip and probe the circuit with the opposite end. It'll prevent your getting any shock. Naturally, hold on to the insulated, shielded part of the device.

Now, here's a big secret. Look at the four items in figure 38.

At left (A), a discarded radio speaker with a condenser clipped to one lead. Next (B), a simple lantern battery with two foot-long, lightweight wires clipped to its negative and positive terminals.

Next in line (C), an everyday, discarded handset from an old phone. This one has an alligator clip fastened to one wire and a probe to the other. For two or three decades until recently, this instrument was really the principal testing device used by *all* professionals. At right (D), is a volt-ohm microammeter (VOM), selling for about $15. Other than the meter, which is really "professional" equipment, the other items are cheap gadgets which can do virtually *everything* in troubleshooting any telephone system problem. An ordinary flashlight dry cell can be used to "test" most telephones.

☎ SPEAKER CLIPPED ACROSS A LINE IT'LL TELL YOU IF THERE'S A DIAL TONE.

☎ BATTERY TOUCHED TO THE ENDS OF THE WIRES FROM A TELEPHONE, THE BATTERY WILL CAUSE A CLICK TO BE HEARD IN THE EARPIECE IF THE SET IS OKAY.

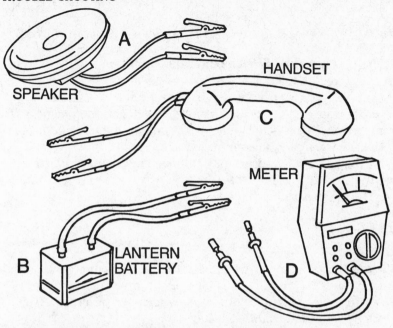

38 / TEST EQUIPMENT SPEAKER, BATTERY, HANDSET, METER

☎ **HANDSET** PROBED INTO A NEW CIRCUIT, IT'LL GIVE YOU THE NICE FAT SOUND OF A DIAL TONE IF THE LINE IS READY FOR USE. CAN BE USED AS AN INTERCOM, SAY, IF YOU'RE ADJUSTING THE DIRECTION OF YOUR TV AERIAL. JUST "TAP" IT ACROSS YOUR HOUSEHOLD PHONE LINES VIA A LONG CORD ON THE ROOF.

☎ **METER** SKIP THE COST AND THE DEVICE UNLESS YOU PLAN TO IM-MERSE YOURSELF IN THIS HOBBY OR BUSINESS. THEN, YOU'LL NEED IT TO MEASURE VOLTAGES, CHECK CONTINUITY OF CIRCUITS, LOCATE "OPENS" OR "SHORTS." IT'S GREAT FUN TO HAVE. START OUT WITH THE CHEAPEST NEW MODEL YOU CAN BUY, MAKE SURE YOU GET AN INSTRUC-TION SHEET WITH IT (OR CHECK OUT AN INSTRUMENTS BOOK FROM YOUR LIBRARY).

Out of curiosity, I inquired at three different TV repair shops (including one general "fix-it" store) what they'd charge to provide all the items pictured (except the meter) in figures 36, 37, and 38.

The bids from the three technicians for a complete "kit" were $10, $12.50, and $16.

I was offered two used meters for $10 each.

In other words, if a person wanted to get into the business of home telephone servicing and installation, he or she might be able to do it for about $25 maximum in tools.

For beginners, however, only the flashlight battery is needed, and then only if you're setting out to buy some garage sale equipment, such as basic telephones. Let's go.

THE TELEPHONE

Whether bought new or used, have the instrument tested before leaving the seller's place of business. Unplug a working phone and plug in the item being sold. If it dials a couple of local numbers correctly, you can assume it's okay.

If you are at a swap meet and there's no access to a phone line, simply tap the telephone wires on the leads from the tiny flashlight battery. If you hear vigorous clicks from the phone earpiece, you can assume the instrument is likely to be okay.

ALL OTHER ACCESSORIES

As with telephones, test accessories before leaving the seller's location, whether buying new or used. You may find that some of the adapters pictured in figure 36 will prove handy for these purposes.

On used equipment, you take your own chances without testing.

WIRING

If you've inherited the wiring installed by the phone company in years past, it's all yours to do with as you wish. It's a smart idea to test each link in the service, whether it's old installation or the new wiring you just installed.

CABLING TEST

1. REMOVE ALL INSTRUMENTS AND ACCESSORIES FROM THE SYSTEM.

2. TOUCH THE LEADS FROM THE BATTERY (ITEM B IN FIGURE 38) QUICKLY, MOMENTARILY, ACROSS THE TWO WIRES OR TERMINALS AT ALL ACCESSIBLE POINTS IN THE SYSTEM. IF YOU SEE A FAINT SPARK, THERE'S A SHORT CIRCUIT SOMEPLACE. SOMEWHERE ALONG THE PATH OF WIRES, THEY'RE CONTACTING EACH OTHER. ISOLATE AND TRACE THE VARIOUS SPANS OF WIRING UNTIL YOU LOCATE IT.

3. NOW PLUG IN A TELEPHONE AT ANY JACK OR MODULAR SOCKET.

4. ASSEMBLE THE TINY SPEAKER WITH THE BATTERY ACROSS ANY POINT IN THE WIRING, THE CLOSER TO THE TERMINAL BOX THE BETTER. SEE FIGURE 39.

5. IF A GOOD TELEPHONE IS PLUGGED INTO A JACK OR SOCKET, YOU'LL HEAR A CLICK WHEN THE BATTERY CONNECTIONS ARE TOUCHED TO THE WIRE. THE SPEAKER WILL MAKE THE SOUND. EVERYTHING'S IN GOOD SHAPE. TO DOUBLE-CHECK, REMOVE THE TELEPHONE AND REPEAT THE TEST. THIS TIME, WHEN YOU TOUCH THE WIRE TO THE BATTERY, THERE'LL BE NO CLICK AND NO SPARK. YOUR WIRING SHOULD BE READY TO USE. RESTORE THE CONNECTIONS OF ALL THE LEGS OF THE CIRCUIT YOU HAVE DISCONNECTED.

Fasten the two wires of your internal phone system to the two connections in the terminal box brought up to your house and wired in place by the phone company.

Plug in your telephone. Hear a dial tone?

Splendid. Phone a friend and say, "You'll never guess what I just did."

If you've traveled deluxe and purchased a meter, as seen in figure 38, you can readily test instruments by removing them from any circuit and placing the meter on the 1,000 ohm (1K) scale. Touch the test probes to the telephone wire ends and then make puffing sounds into the telephone mouthpiece. Your wheezes should send the meter needle zapping up and down.

Inside the handset is the magnetic-dynamic earphone which reproduces sounds by the motion of its diaphragm back and forth according to the electrical impulses that reach its nearby magnetic coils. The transmitter, or mouthpiece, is a tiny metal box full of carbon dust. The lid of the box is also a flexible diaphragm cover that moves back and forth with the pressures of the speaker's voice. The carbon dust in the box is thus compressed and relaxed, sent convulsing into frantic configurations that change the resist-

ance values between the poles (conductors) fastened to the box.
Unscrew the mouthpiece on a handset. The transmitter will probably fall out into your hand. It'll add to your know-how about telephones.

1–REMOVE PHONE
2–INSERT HANDSET OR RADIO SPEAKER
3–LISTEN FOR DIAL TONE

OR

TEST EACH MODULAR POINT IN SEQUENCE.
LIFTING WIRES TO NEXT CONNECTOR AS YOU GO.

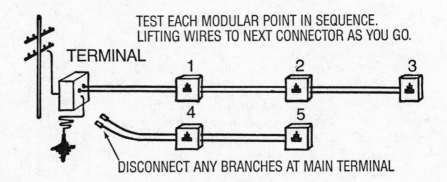

TERMINAL

DISCONNECT ANY BRANCHES AT MAIN TERMINAL

OR

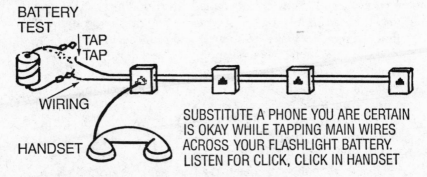

BATTERY
TEST

TAP
TAP

WIRING

HANDSET

SUBSTITUTE A PHONE YOU ARE CERTAIN
IS OKAY WHILE TAPPING MAIN WIRES
ACROSS YOUR FLASHLIGHT BATTERY.
LISTEN FOR CLICK, CLICK IN HANDSET

39 / TEST ASSEMBLY ANOTHER WAY TO TROUBLE SHOOT

MOST OFTEN ENCOUNTERED TROUBLES

IMPORTANT NOTE: In the new system of phone service, you can be cheerfully honest about everything relating to your phone service. The repair operator will appreciate knowing what you've done and your information will speed up the location of the problem in the central office or in the lines between the central and your location.

NO DIAL TONE

You can't call out. Also, you can't be reached. Is the fault in your equipment or in Ma's?

1. TRY EACH PHONE IN YOUR SYSTEM. MAYBE ONLY ONE IS A "NO-TONE."

2. NO? THEN UNPLUG EACH ACCESSORY AND LISTEN TO HEAR IF A DIAL TONE RETURNS IN THE REMAINING SETS OR YOUR TEST SET.

3. NO? THEN, TO DETERMINE IF THE PROBLEM IS A SHORT OR OPEN IN *YOUR* WIRING OR THE PHONE COMPANY'S, "LIFT" (DISCONNECT) THE WIRES WHERE YOU ATTACHED THEM TO THE ENTRY TERMINAL BOX. CLIP YOUR TEST HANDSET (WITH THE ALLIGATOR CLIPS) ACROSS THE PHONE COMPANY'S WIRES. DIAL TONE? IF YES, THE PROBLEM *MUST* BE IN YOUR INSTALLATION. IF NO DIAL TONE AT THIS JUNCTION, PHONE THE REPAIR SERVICE OFFICE AND ASK THEM TO LOCATE THE PROBLEM IN THEIR LINES FROM CENTRAL OFFICE.

4. IF YOU DID HAVE A DIAL TONE AT THE ENTRY TERMINAL, YOU'LL HAVE TO CHECK THE WIRING AT EACH TERMINAL IN THE SYSTEM. THE OPEN OR SHORT IS FIRST ASSUMED TO EXIST BETWEEN THE ENTRY TERMINAL AND YOUR *FIRST* PHONE CONNECTOR.

5. IF THE DIAL TONE CAN BE HEARD AT THE FIRST TERMINAL THEN PRO-CEED ALONG TO YOUR OTHER EXTENSION TERMINALS, ISOLATING EACH UNTIL THE FAULTY WIRING OR SOCKET CONNECTION IS FOUND.

MORE TROUBLE—YOU'RE TOLD YOU CAN'T BE CALLED

Friends, relatives, or neighbors tell you in person that your line must be out of order. Maybe they've been getting the routine "out of service" recorded message, or hours of busy signals.

Before inviting the repair service out for a costly service call, follow the procedure outlines for no dial tone. It can save you bagfuls of money.

CALLS ARE FULL OF STATIC, NOISE, AND CRACKLING

If the condition persists beyond a few hours, simply disconnect the wires at the terminal box, clip in a substitute telephone and make a call. If it's still noisy, the problem belongs to the phone company. It's their task to fix the line to central without charge.

But if the call is now clear, start looking in your own system for loose connections, frayed wires, wobbly plugs, or tired instruments. Clean the hook switch contacts inside the instrument. Simply drag a strip of bond paper between the contacts.

As usual, the best way to check telephone instruments is by *substitution*. Plug your equipment into a neighbor's modular socket and see if it works well there.

Or, borrow a neighbor's good telephone and connect it throughout your system. The resulting sounds should lead you quickly to the trouble area. The socket that causes the racket may have a loose, corroded, or shorting wire connection.

BASE CORD TROUBLES

Frayed and tired wires will cause noisy, static-crackly calls.

Twist the instrument's wires along their lengths to the connector on the wall.

When you come to any section where the internal conductors are creating problems, you'll know it. If the crackling doesn't get worse, the set will probably simply go dead.

Before discarding the whole cord, try attaching a different wire or wires within the sheath.

Replacement wires from any terminal to the base of phone or handset are relatively cheap. But when you open the base of the phone, take your time, replace the connecting wires one by one, maintaining the color coding.

RINGER TROUBLES

If you determine that one of your telephones is a-okay except it refuses to ring, locate the ringing condenser (see Part Four, figure 40). It's usually the culprit. A replacement condenser can be bought for twenty-five cents. Or maybe easier—sometimes the ringing circuit has simply been disconnected or turned to "off." Check the lever or thumb switch in the base of the phone.

DIALS AND PADS

Contrary to some expert opinion, telephone rotary dials can often go sour, always making the same mistake, maybe connecting you with the same wrong number every time you dial. It'll hardly be worth repairing because surely, by this time it'll have made millions upon millions of switching pulses. Save the telephone for spare parts, but remove it from service. The handset should make a dandy test monitor.

Pushbutton phones will occasionally go on the rampage. The reason? Each number on the tone pad generates two frequencies or tone sounds when it's depressed. Sometimes, though rarely, one of the frequencies will simply quit. You can still hear a sound when you press the buttons, but it'll take an expert to detect the absence of a single tone. There are basically only seven frequencies in the tone system. Each digit combines a different pair of them.

If a pushbutton phone consistently gives you wrong numbers (the same or variable numbers) and fails in a substitution test, take it out of service, using it selectively for spare parts.

BELL TAP

If your system includes all rotary dial phones or a mixture of dials and pushbuttons, sometimes the "bell" will tap on an extension when another phone is being dialed. Most of the time the annoyance can be corrected by reversing the base phone connections or the "tapper" (the hammer that strikes the bell in response to pulses of electricity). If not, adjust the spring tension on the tapper.

☎ SUMMARY

The chapter has surely covered more than 95 percent of the problems that beset most telephones, residential systems, and central offices. Consider right now that you probably have enough equipment and know-how to avoid forever even one expensive service call from any phone company. And that's a fact!

PART FOUR

An Inside Look at Things Present and Future

9 IN CASE
YOU WANT TO SOUND
LIKE A PRO

Figure 40 reveals the inner parts of a standard telephone.

All instruments are essentially the same on the inside. Snoopy® has the same innards as Mickey Mouse® now that they've both become popular figures.

Different manufacturers use different types of base plates. The numbers that are imprinted on these plates vary from unit to unit. In one telephone, if you open up the case, you might find a red conductor clipped on to a terminal numbered 14. On the next phone, the same terminal might bear the number 45. The words of caution are provided here for the individual who, say, is changing the base cord. Remove old wires and snap on new ones artfully. One wire at a time, please.

There are springs that lift the hook switch when the receiver is lifted. Other springs control the tensions on the tapper. The other hardware includes diodes, straps, coils, and assorted switches that are just about the same in all phones made during the past half century.

We can get an idea of how calls are completed, in and out of your residence.

INCOMING CALLS

When the central office receives a call for you, the electro-mechanical or digital switches close on the two wires leading to your resi-

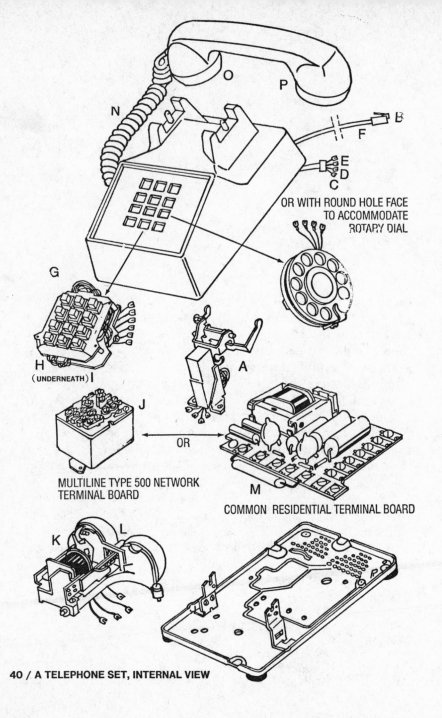

OR WITH ROUND HOLE FACE
TO ACCOMMODATE
ROTARY DIAL

G

H
(UNDERNEATH)

A

J

OR

MULTILINE TYPE 500 NETWORK
TERMINAL BOARD

M

COMMON RESIDENTIAL TERMINAL BOARD

K   L

40 / A TELEPHONE SET, INTERNAL VIEW

dence. A blip of alternating current is shot down the line, past your terminal and into your incoming cord (F). It zips past the modular connector (B) and scoots through that section of the hook switch (A) which is being held in correct position by the weight of the handset. Depending on your system, the current will be fluctuating at a rate of twenty-five cycles per second (there are a dozen frequencies in general use). The central office equipment sends one-second pulses with four-second pauses in between. The current is enough to scramble through the wiring, usually taking the routes through red (C) and yellow (E). Often the yellow wire and green wire (D) will be plugged on to the same terminal. The pulse of electricity slams into the condenser (M) which blocks the direct current component on the line and allows the alternating current to reach the finger coil. In this way, the ringer coil (K) is magnetized on and off to attract and repel the bell tapper (L) from side to side, to ring your bell. The loudness of the bell is often controlled by the amount of tension on the spring which is adjustable by lever or wheel peeking out through the base of the phone. Remember, during all of this time, there's another voltage (direct current), already squatting on that same pair of lines, just itching to get into action. The power is supplied from a monstrous storage battery at central. The battery is a mammoth version of the one that starts your car.

Well, you hear the bell which usually rings just when you get in the shower or bath. You dash to the telephone and lift the receiver, stretching the handset cord (N). But before that cord has even wiggled, the weight removal causes the hook switch (A) to flip to its other correct position. The ringing voltage is immediately cut off back at central. Only the direct current remains "on line."

You say "hello" into the transmitter (O) of the handset and the sound is transposed from air motion to electrical activity in the transmitter back along the wires to your own phone and that of your caller. Zap, zing, whish!

A HOOK SWITCH. B INCOMING MODULAR. C RING CONNECTOR (USUALLY RED). D TIP CONNECTOR (USUALLY GREEN). E GROUND LEAD (USUALLY YELLOW). F INCOMING CORD. G PUSH-BUTTON PAD. H CRYSTAL CONTROLLER. I TONE GENERATOR. J INDUCTION COIL. K BELL AND RINGER COIL. L BELL TAPPER. M RINGER CONDENSER. N HANDSET CORD. O TRANSMITTER. P EARPIECE (RECEIVER).

As you start talking, the tiny, dustlike granules of carbon within the transmitter are blapped around between the incoming and outgoing connectors, one of which is connected to a flexible diaphram or "lid on the box."

WHILE YOU'RE TALKING, THINGS ARE HAPPENING

Each inflection, breath, word, causes the carbon granules to compress and relax in accordance with the in-and-out movements of the diaphragm on the little carbon containers. As the carbon dust slams every which way within the boxes, the resistance to electricity is changing. Thus, the amount and shape of audio frequency voltage is being changed as it scrams back and forth along the direct current path that now exists on the wires between your phone and that of your caller. And those frequencies are of an alternating type which are simultaneously slipping through the primary windings of the tiny induction coil (J). There are two voltages now present in that coil and they get together to flow out along the wires. The coil is simply a mini-spool of two ultrafine wires. The fluctuations of voltage on the inner spool (primary) cause changes on the wiring wrapped around it (secondary) and a smidgeon of that current is called the sidetone which is fed back into the earpiece and is a tiny "dynamic" listening device.

The foregoing description will drive most telephone engineers into a state of hysteria because they'd use much longer words. If you'd like to learn those words, the best place to apply is your local community college, most of which conduct regular and extension courses in telephony. I hope by now you've begun to realize that telephone things are every bit as interesting and important as other utilities and facilities in our lives.

Meanwhile, at the central office, if your call is on a toll or long-distance basis, a mini-section of the revenue computer is counting off the seconds as you yak-yak-yak, standing there fresh from the shower. If you have a hunch the central office locations are maintained under tight security, you can believe that the computers that measure the billing time of your basic service and toll calls are maintained tighter than Fort Knox. There are so many interlocks, security-fixes, electronic, manual, and human guards hovering over the *revenue computers* that nothing, but nothing on earth could ever disturb them, short of world chaos.

SO—YOU DECIDE TO MAKE A CALL TO SOMEONE ELSE

You lift the receiver which activates the hook switch (A) and that action sends some switches into spasms at central. This time, however, you hear that familiar dial tone which lets you know your two lines are intact and that appropriate voltages are floating along your wires waiting for work. If you have a rotary phone, you'll begin dialing and the mini-switch inside the handset will click the voltages *off* and *on* ten times a second in accord with the numbers you dial. The pushbutton phone, however, will have cranked up its pad (G) to start generating seven tones through a crystal controlled oscillator circuit (H) and frequency generator (I).

Each numbered button you push squirts a pair of frequency tones back through the wires, around the induction coils in and out of other parts, then back to your central office.

As fast as the tones are received, they're sorted.

The relay at central says, "Hey, here's a *three* and a *four* and wow, a *nine*. That's the central office downtown. Go, baby, go!"

And instantly, that prefix lands in its own area station waiting for you to tell it which of the 9,999 available numbers in that 349 area you're going to pushbutton next.

The whole rigamarole is repeated hundreds of millions of times each day.

If you'd like a little exercise in creative thinking, just imagine what the whole world would be like if suddenly, say in the very next minute, every telephone would vanish. Think of the incredible possibilities that would occur in political, business, domestic, and family affairs. Without those two phone lines from point to point, life as we know it, would become almost insufferable within a matter of hours.

EXPLORING YOUR ANSWERING MACHINE

Don't.

No matter whose machine you buy, your chances of taking it apart and giving it any restoration service are very unlikely. There are simply too many multifunction relays, diodes, transistors, mos-fets, zeners, flip-flops, and other such neat technical names for any real person to cope with. Expert technicians despise them. They have inner workings that only their manufacturers can love.

They should run along quite happily with routine care.

If, however, you don't follow your owner's handbook and carry out the regular rituals of dusting the machines, cleaning up the recording heads as the manufacturer describes the process, et cetera, you'll soon own trash instead of treasure.

ALL OTHER TELEPHONE ACCESSORIES

Despite the basic simplicity of most telephone add-ons, they are usually identifiable under one of two categories:

1. They're made so sturdily and thoughtfully that it's almost impossible for them to get out of whack. Or—

2. They've been assembled so cheaply and hurriedly that they become a pain in the ear.

Let me give you an example of the second category. I have a telephone on which I can actually dial numbers by simply whumping it up and down on the table, turning it upside down to separate digits. I keep it as an oddity, sort of a house pet.

Cautions: Many manufacturers, even Ma Bell herself, can make errors in manufacturing things. A good example is the early model of the Princess phone which was so light in weight that the user had to hold the base firmly in one hand while dialing the stupid thing with the other. Ma made a few hundred thousand of them before realizing her manufacturing folks had better make the bases heavier.

If, when buying equipment, you have a choice between a hefty model and a lightweight thing, go for the heavy one. The chance of getting better quality seems to have a relationship to weight in the telephone biz. I'm not suggesting one should buy phones, dialers, and such things by the pound. But having seen some of the super-quality equipment pouring in to the USA from the most unlikely places, like Haiti, Sri Lanka, Portugal, and Ireland, places that we don't regularly associate with high technology, I'm obliged to urge caution upon you.

Those same countries are also sending us penny-a-pound junk.

KEEPING MA BELL AT A DISTANCE:
ALTERNATIVE LONG-DISTANCE TELEPHONE SERVICES

If you want to sound like a pro you better know bits and pieces about the new alternatives in long-distance dialing. Way back in 1963, a little company called MCI (then it meant Microwave Communications, Inc.) started filing requests for permission from the FCC to operate a simple microwave service between Chicago and St. Louis.

Ma Bell had a fit! She fought the whole idea! It took years but finally, the little David (MCI) whumped the lights out of Goliath (AT&T, Ma's former bodyguard, some would say, pimp). MCI won permission and AT&T's choke hold on communications was broken, at least temporarily.

MCI did so well at reducing long-distance charges that other companies tried to get into the act. There were some failures. Some of the companies, notably Hart of Florida, required a deposit to get into their service. When the company went into bankruptcy, a lot of nice people lost their "up front" money.

As of the winter of 1982 there were only five companies other than AT&T in the business on anything that might resemble a national scale. Smaller companies are breeding like rabbits.

☎ "LONGER DISTANCE" (FORMERLY CITY CALL) IS A SPIN-OFF OF ITT IN NEW YORK, THROUGH ITS UNITED STATES TRANSMISSION SYSTEMS, INC.

☎ MCI IS A WASHINGTON-BASED SPECIALTY CORPORATION, VERY CENTRALIZED IN PHOENIX, AZ.

☎ SPRINT IS OWNED BY GENERAL TELEPHONE COMPANY, IF FCC APPROVES. MAJOR OPERATIONS IN DETROIT.

☎ METROFONE IS AN OFFSPRING OF WESTERN UNION.

☎ SBS (SATELLITE BUSINESS SYSTEMS) IS A JOINT VENTURE OF IBM, AETNA INSURANCE, AND COMSAT. QUARTERED IN VIRGINIA.

AT&T is the former one and only heavyweight.

Are the newcomers better than the Giant? You decide for yourself. Never forget that even in the divestiture process, AT&T never relaxed its grip on the high profit long-distance operations and of course there are residual connections that shall forever remain like old love letters between AT&T and its twenty-two Bell Telephone Companies, now being scattered.

The "new" systems require that you call or write them to open an account. From New York and most other regions you can reach some of these companies toll-free. Longer Distance: (800) 526-3000. MCI: (800) 528-0613. Metrofone: (800) 325-6000. SBS: (Skyline): (800) 235-2001. Sprint: (800) 521-4949. These numbers sometimes change in other area codes. In Canada, the TransCanada Telephone System will provide a continent-wide service beginning mid-1983, a joint venture with MCI of the United States.

If you haven't got a pushbutton phone you'll need one for openers. Your credit background data is equally of interest. You'll get an access code and account number and theoretically have the capability at once of making cheaper long-distance calls. You'll simply dial your local Longer Distance, MCI, Sprint, Metrofone or Skyline number and then when the system replies, you'll punch in your multidigit access number. Then you'll perhaps be queried for your account number and if your account number is current, the computer will signal you to proceed. You go ahead, using your local phone line which ties into their microwave or satellite hook-ups.

If you routinely used AT&T, the foregoing steps would have been handled automatically by Ma Bell. Basically, as the newcomers have been saying, if your long-distance calls have been topping $25 a month, you'll probably save money by switching away from AT&T. You can be sure that AT&T isn't taking that kind of news lying down.

Of course, Ma Bell is reminding us that the competitors might be able to long-distance you from major city to major city. But just try to get a long-distance call to some offbeat little town. No chance! There are some subscribers who say that if you can't dial dear old Grandfather in No Chance, just wait'll you hear the static and flawed calls when you try to reach Mom in Miami.

The chart on page 128—129 will show you the cost among five contenders in the Long-Distance Tournament. At best it's a sample of charges for different times from Chicago to six major cities. All of the services offer discount and package rates that might waggle the figures a penny or two. But it's a starting point!

Well, what do you think? Will you stick with Ma or kiss her good-bye?

The decision is yours.

The important point that can't be emphasized too strongly in this book or anyplace else is that now, for the first time, in communications, you have some choices.

If you really want to learn a lot about your area's phone company, read the vitally important data presented at the front and back ends of your telephone directory. Usually both the white pages and yellow pages are crammed with interesting reading about your system and how it purports to work.

THE BOTTOM LINE

By virtue of their monopolistic positioning, Bell Telephone companies, like the gas, electric, and metropolitan transit companies, have had to work under the guidelines determined by public utility commissions. These commissions are usually made up of individuals appointed by state governors or lesser elected officials.

When rate hikes have been requested, the PUCs, as they're called, usually schedule hearings at which civilians can converse with utility professionals. But commissioners are dunned and courted by the lawyers and persuaders of utility companies every day and night of every year.

Now that they're all being "deregulated," we are hearing promises that the competitive factors of a "free market" will hold prices in check, but competition alone may not be effective without your participation.

Obviously, it would be unproductive to have several phone companies franchised for every area because you could then contact only those individuals using the same system. One answer that is proving to be tremendously effective has been to assure phone companies—and other utilities—a way to maintain healthy service

COMPARISON CHART OF COST PER MINUTE**

CHICAGO TO:	MA BELL/AT&T				CITY CALL (ITT) "LONGER DISTANCE"		MCI "EXECUNET"	
	11 P.M.-8 A.M. & WEEKENDS 1ST MIN.	EA. ADD'L MIN.	SUN.-THURS. 5 P.M.-11 P.M. 1ST MIN.	EA. ADD'L MIN.	11 P.M.-8 A.M. & WEEKENDS	MON.-FRI. 5 P.M.-11 P.M.	11 P.M.-8 A.M. MON.-FRI.	SUN.-FRI. 5 P.M.-11 P.M.
BOSTON	29¢	20¢	37¢	26¢	13¢	15¢	16¢	20¢
DENVER	25	18	38	27	11	15	13	17
LOS ANGELES	25	18	38	27	11	16	14	18
MIAMI	25	18	38	27	11	15	14	18
NEW YORK	24	17	37	26	11	15	14	17
SEATTLE	24	17	39	27	11	15	14	18

*NS = Designates no service to this area
**To nearest penny.

at justifiable rates. This has been done with Citizen's Utility Boards (CUBs), which have been particularly successful in Wisconsin but are already growing like wildfire nationally. There is probably something comparable starting to form in your community, wherever you live, because we, the people, have become increasingly concerned about runaway tariffs in all utility systems.

The Wisconsin CUB was established by referendum in 1982 and within months of its formation was barely able to keep abreast of applications for membership. In October 1982 there were more than 60,000 ratepayers supporting the efforts of only 10 staff members who claimed they'd saved phone, gas and electric users more than *one hundred million dollars* in excessive charges within the first year of operation. Expectedly, the utility companies deny such claims. But right or wrong, for the first time, the people who pay the bills are being represented by lawyers who can confront the companies' lawyers and lobbyists in front of Public Utility Commissions.

CHARGES OFFERED BY VARIOUS TELEPHONE SERVICES

METROFONE		SPRINT (GTE)		SBS "SKYLINE"	
11 P.M.-8 A.M. & WEEKENDS	7 DAYS 6 P.M.-11 P.M.	11 P.M.-8 A.M. & WEEKENDS	MON.-FRI. 5 P.M.-11 P.M.	Unlike others, Skyline charges by area rather than distance.	
				DAILY ANY NEIGHBORING STATE 11 P.M.-8 A.M.	DAILY ANY OTHER STATE
12¢	17¢	15¢	18¢	10¢	14¢
12	17	15	18	8 A.M.-5 P.M. 25¢	39¢
13	18	16	20	5 P.M.-11 P.M. 13¢	18¢
12	17	15	18	$16 to initiate the service, *first* time you call out on it.	
12	17	14	18		
12	17	16	20		

Note: Residential rates for SBS (Satellite Business Systems) not available at press time.

Don't overload the staff of Wisconsin CUB but if you'd like to hear how they are doing, contact them: Citizens Utility Board, 301 East Johnson Street, Madison, Wisconsin 53703.

If you can't locate a CUB type of group in your community, you might want to form your own, from scratch. The Ralph Nader organization may already have a representative in your neighborhood. If not, ask for free start-up help from Telecommunications Research Center, Box 12038, Washington, D.C. 20005.

Although this book has been dedicated to the nuts and bolts of buying and installing your own telephone and accessories, you'll still be paying charges each month to maintain those two wires to central offices. You can't get away from Ma Bell completely, and maintaining a healthy utility company, charging equitable rates, requires the same kind of concern you showed in learning to install your own equipment. For your self-protection you'll simply have to do it yourself! A CUB program is one way of becoming involved.

APPENDICES

APPENDIX A

STEP-BY-STEP INSTALLATION WITHOUT APPROVED CONNECTORS

1 Assemble your tools, mostly a medium-size screwdriver, a sharp knife, some electrical tape (please, no masking tape or cellophane tape, eh?) and, if you can get one, a soldering iron.

2 Use existing wires and terminals wherever possible, leaving the main entry terminal disconnected. Then, if you can't resist, add on your extra wiring from point to point. Your wire simply *must* have two insulated conductors, right?

3 Test your various telephone sets and accessories. Ask a friend for permission to touch the two (or more) connections from all of your gadgets across any dial tone circuit that he or she has at home. The battery test is a good one but a nice, fat dial tone is much better.

4 With your sharp knife, carefully remove the insulation at all points where you plan to hook up a telephone or accessory. Scratch away all the dirt and corrosion.

5 If you're still going "dirt poor" with pigtail wire ends on your instruments, give them a thorough cleaning, too.

6 By twisting or wrapping or soldering, even *binding* with a finer wire, strive to get a sturdy mechanical connection between one wire of the equipment to one wire of the phone system. Add one of the "continuing" wires to the same position, again striving for a good mechanical as well as electrical bond. Tape the joint, snugly.

7 Proceed to hook up the second wire. Usually, if it's a telephone handset and you want it to ring, you'll fasten the yellow and green wires together on one line, the red, by itself, to the other. You can be certain only by testing as discussed on page 40. As before, add on the continuing conductor. Solder the bunch together and tape snugly.

8 At each step in your installation, momentarily connect the two wires at the terminals on the main entry box. If you've paid Ma Bell and she's provided you with a dial tone you should hear it loud and clear at your newly acquired and wired telephone.

9 Proceed in the same fashion to wire in other phones and accessories, testing each addition as you go by temporarily hooking up and then unfastening the wires at the main terminal.

10 This connect/disconnect process reduces the possibility of feeling a little nip of electricity if someone happens to ring in while you're holding on to the two bare wire ends. Also, it safeguards the entry box if your soldering iron or some other unexpected source zaps out spikes of high voltage.

As mentioned earlier, the ringing voltage, though high, carries very little current. At the central office there's a "ballast," not unlike an electric light bulb that senses any oddball conditions out there in Phoneland. It instantly reduces the power to prevent any damage to equipment or amateur installers, like us.

Good luck! Enjoy yourself!

APPENDIX B

STEP-BY-STEP INSTALLATION USING APPROVED CONNECTORS

1 Having surveyed your location you've bought the approved cabling, preferably six-conductor, 22- or 24-gauge plus the wall mount or surface mount terminals for the several locations where you plan to install phones or accessories at a present or future date.

2 No matter whether your equipment is new or used, pre-test all of it in the modular connectors of a friend's telephone service.

3 By this time you'll have decided whether to use existing wiring and terminals and simply "add-on" new cabling or start over from scratch. If practical for you, install the cabling using round-head approved staples and a round-headed staple gun. Call a tool rental shop if you don't wish to buy one.

4 Follow your survey sketch and begin cabling, hiding the wire behind moulding, inside walls and under carpeting if you can locate areas of low or zero foot traffic.

5 The most convenient sockets for most amateurs are those that can be wired under screws. Maintain your color coding as you move along from socket to socket. For reassurance, clip your cabling into place at the main entry point and if the dial tone is on your line, call a friend or use a free service like "Time" to make a call and check your installations.

6 If you've decided to "go the whole distance," the supply department of your local phone company will have sold you their quick-connect/disconnect terminals and the $5 tool which enables you to press the connectors into place without even removing the plastic insulation.

7 With all the working equipment in place, fasten your connections at the main terminal box, looping the wires under the washers and nuts in a clockwise direction.

Now, relax and tell yourself how smart you are!

APPENDIX C

CLEANING AND RENUMBERING PHONES

Telephone instruments usually respond shiny bright to vigorous applications of soap and water applied and scrubbed with a damp sponge. There are plastic polishes that can help scour away scratches and stains.

On rotary dial instruments, the face plate can be removed in order to change the old number. Simply spin the dial clockwise until the 0 fingerhole reaches the fingerstop. Turn it past the stop, usually about one quarter inch. You'll feel it snub up against a lock tab. Now unbend a small paper clip and press the point down through the tiny hole just inside the fingerhole for 0 and press the lock tab down. A hint of additional clockwise turning and the face plate should pop out into your hand. Clean finger path.

Type your new numbers and area code on a card and set it in place behind the face plate, being careful that the numbers will read easily when the plate is back in position.

Lower the face plate gently into position, twisting it slightly counterclockwise if necessary until it snaps back into position.

If the tiny "paper clip hole" isn't apparent on your handset, you may have to dismantle the dial from the inside out.

On pushbutton phones, most face plates can be pried upward gently with a knife or the entire outer shell can be lifted by removing the holding screw in its base. Go gently, please.

APPENDIX D

PHONE BILL INFORMATION

You're interested in the costs of telephone service aren't you? Your telephone bill may not tell you. Over the years, the practice of "bundling" charges has served to conceal tariffs for this utility.

If your local company doesn't *unbundle* its monthly bills, start hounding the public utilities commission for your area to insist on getting to the facts.

You may discover that your "basic monthly service charge" might be including the basic access (your two connecting lines for dial tone) plus such little nifties as a charge for an arbitrary basic minimum of "free calls," which you may not ever use, plus, perhaps, rental for the wiring in your location, plus, perhaps, an extra tariff because of a pushbutton phone "special line" or buzzers and ding-dongs which have long ceased to be in your system.

An example may be the home where two lines were once brought onto the premises until one was subsequently disconnected. The "access line" charge might have been deleted by the computer but frequently the accessories, such as lights and disconnect switches, are still being charged against the remaining line.

Phone your local business office and get an item-by-item accounting.

And never hesitate to challenge local toll charges and unfamiliar long-distance billings. In other words, do your own unbundling if your local phone company seems unwilling to do it as a regular practice.

APPENDIX E

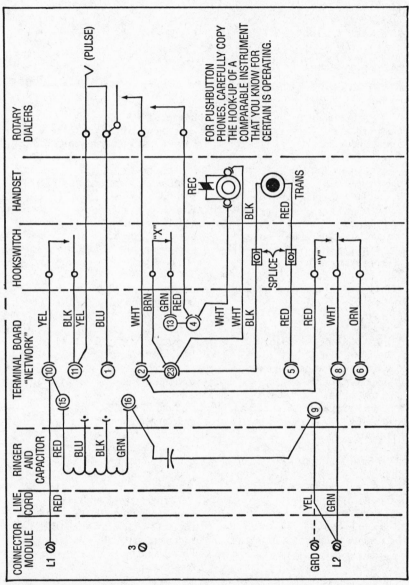

TYPICAL WIRING DIAGRAM TO GUIDE YOU IN CONNECTING MOST (BUT NOT ALL)
TELEPHONE SETS